Using History to Develop Problem-solving and Thinking Skills at Key Stage 2

Edited by
Belle Wallace

David Fulton Publishers
London

David Fulton Publishers Ltd
The Chiswick Centre, 414 Chiswick High Road, London W4 5TF

www.fultonpublishers.co.uk

David Fulton Publishers is a division of Granada Learning Limited, part of the Granada Media group.

First published in Great Britain by David Fulton Publishers 2003
10 9 8 7 6 5 4 3 2 1

British Library Cataloguing in Publication Data
A catalogue record for this book is available from the British Library

ISBN 1-85346-928-9

Designed and typeset by Kate Williams, Abergavenny
Printed and bound in Great Britain by Ashford Colour Press Ltd. Gosport, Hants

**THE NATIONAL ASSOCIATION FOR
ABLE CHILDREN IN EDUCATION
NACE National Office, PO Box 242
Arnolds Way, Oxford OX2 9FR**

Registered Charity No. 327230

Tel: 01865 861879   **Fax: 01865 861880**
e-mail: info@nace.co.uk   **www.nace.co.uk**

MISSION STATEMENT

NACE . . . the association of professionals, promoting and supporting the education of able, gifted and talented children and young people.

AIMS

1. To promote the fact that able, gifted and talented children and young people have particular educational needs, which must be met to realise their full potential.

2. To be proactive in promoting discussion and debate by raising appropriate issues in all education forums and through liaison with educational policy makers.

3. To encourage commitment to the personal, social and intellectual development of the whole child or young person.

4. To encourage a broad, balanced and appropriate curriculum for the able, gifted and talented.

5. To encourage the use of differentiated educational provision in the classroom through curriculum enrichment and extension.

6. To make education an enjoyable, exciting and worthwhile experience for the able, gifted and talented child.

OBJECTIVES

1. To promote the development, implementation and evaluation in all schools and colleges of a coherent policy for able, gifted and talented children and young people.

2. To provide appropriate support, resources and materials for the education of the able, gifted and talented.

3. To provide methods of identification and support to the education community.

4. To provide and facilitate appropriate initial teacher training and continuing professional development for teachers and school leaders.

5. To facilitate research activities.

Contents ○ ● ○ ○

Notes on Contributors

Belle Wallace has worked with very able children for over 25 years, first in an advisory capacity to Essex schools; then as a researcher and developer of a problem-solving and thinking skills base for curriculum development. She maintains that the performance levels of all pupils can be raised when they are systematically taught a range of thinking skills, and she has developed curricula internationally for disadvantaged learners. Since its inception in 1982, she has been editor of the journal *Gifted Education International*. She has published widely, served on the Executive Board of the World Council for Gifted and Talented Children (WCGTC), and is currently President of the National Association for Able Children in Education, UK (NACE). Her particular interest is in working with teachers to develop their expertise in the teaching of problem-solving and thinking skills across the National Curriculum. She has edited a series of practical classroom based texts for the teaching of thinking skills at early years, primary and middle years published by David Fulton Publishers in association with NACE.

Diana Cave began her teaching career in middle schools in Warwickshire and for the past 13 years has taught in The National School, Grantham, Lincolnshire. During this time she has held a number of consecutive posts with special responsibility, namely: Year 3 Team Leader coordinating work across the year and liaising with local infant schools; Year 6 Team Leader; Assessment Coordinator and Curriculum Coordinator. She has consequently acquired a unique range of experience across both subject areas and year groups. She was one of the major contributors to *Teaching Thinking Skills Across the Primary Curriculum: A practical approach for all abilities* (Wallace 2001) published by David Fulton Publishers in association with NACE.

Joy Bentley combines her part-time work for Worcestershire LEA in the dual role of Teacher Adviser for History and for More Able Children. Before this she acquired a wide range of teaching and management experience in secondary, middle and first schools. Her interest in problem-solving and thinking skills has developed in tandem with her love of history and the potential it has for developing the skills of enquiry and for enthusing children with an interest in their historical heritage.

Peter Riches is head teacher of Gonerby Hill Foot Church of England (CE) Primary School in Grantham, Lincolnshire. He has taught widely in primary education over the last 25 years, and has a particular interest in history. In addition, he has contributed to the teacher education programmes at Bishop Grosseteste and Harlaxton Colleges, and is presently involved in an international school leadership project.

Tricia McLean studied psychology at the University of Birmingham and went on to qualify as a primary school teacher at the University of London, Institute of Education. She worked as an infant teacher for a number of years in a school in SE London. While taking time out to have four children, she gained a qualification in Counselling. For the last five years, she has taught at Gonerby Hill Foot CE Primary School in Grantham, Lincolnshire where she is Special Needs Coordinator.

Richard Scott qualified as a secondary school teacher in design and ceramics and physical education at St Paul's College of Physical Education in 1977, before joining the RAF as a physical training instructor in the same year. He specialised in parachute training and gained a commission as a physical education officer in 1986. When he left the RAF in 1994, he re-trained as a primary school teacher at Huddersfield University. He has since taught throughout Key Stage 2 at Gonerby Hill Foot CE Primary School, Grantham, Lincolnshire where his responsibilities include coordinating science and PE/games.

Selecia Chapman began her teaching career working with the Foundation Years but now works with Key Stage 2 children. She is Senior Teacher at Billingborough Primary School, Lincolnshire and has a special interest in history. She sees the teaching of history as a vehicle for developing children's interest in and enthusiasm for their heritage, as well as a means of developing their problem-solving and research skills. She also sees history as the means of developing a holistic way of learning encompassing the full range of children's multiple intelligences.

Sheila Woodhead graduated from Madeley College of Education and has taught in Boston and Pinchbeck in Lincolnshire. She has taught extensively in Key Stage 1 and 2 and is particularly interested in developing children's writing skills.

Acknowledgements

I would like to thank Harvey B. Adams with whom I worked to research and develop a generic and sound theoretical framework for the development of problem-solving and thinking skills across the curriculum. We spent 15 years working mainly with disadvantaged learners across the world in order to derive a problem-solving paradigm that really worked in practice to lift learners' levels of achievement so that they had the opportunity to maximise their potential and take their rightful place in the world. Teaching learners strategies for thinking encourages very able learners to develop tools for independent learning so that they can pursue topics to greater depth and breadth. However, a thinking skills framework also gives average ability children the necessary support to improve the level of their performance.

I would particularly like to thank Diana Cave who, over a number of years, has provided leadership and encouragement to her colleagues enabling them to work in depth to trial the TASC (Thinking Actively in a Social Context) Problem-solving Model across a wide range of selected topics in the National Curriculum. My thanks also to Joy Bentley, Tricia McLean, Richard Scott, Selecia Chapman and Sheila Woodhead who have contributed to this text through planning, teaching and evaluating a number of topics taken from the Framework for Teaching History which they have interpreted using the TASC approach. Thanks also to Peter Riches who researched the websites and publishers in order to create the resource list. I am grateful to Kate Waghorn of Barrowby CE Primary School, who took the photographs of the school's celebration of Victorian times.

The following head teachers facilitated and encouraged their members of staff by being willing to accommodate their need for time and flexibility:

- John Gibbs: The National School, Lincs

- Peter Riches: Gonerby Hill Foot CE Primary School, Lincs

- Julie Harrison: Billingborough Primary School, Lincs

- Cheryl Baumber: Pinchbeck East CE Primary School, Lincs

Sylvia West: Barrowby CE Primary School, Lincs, kindly gave permission to use the school photographs.

And, finally, thanks to all the children who participated in the projects. They were excited to try new ideas and ways of working and showed their enthusiasm in their motivation to work in their own time using great initiative and determination.

Preface

The Programme of Study for history allows great freedom in designing learning experiences for Key Stage 2 pupils. Admittedly, there is a limiting time factor – often too little time for pupils to explore in depth and breadth but we are encouraged to make selections of appropriate topics. Moreover, if we aim to incorporate a wide range of quality activities over the whole school year, then we can effectively build up a repertoire of problem-solving activities and thinking skills through a wide range of interesting and motivating tasks. In addition, when learners are keen and interested it is not difficult to encourage out of school learning and to promote exciting activities through a history club.

If we extrapolate and interpret the key elements from the Programme of Study, then we have the essence of a problem-solving and thinking skills curriculum. In addition, we have the essential components of a curriculum which fosters emotional and social intelligence. Using a wide range of activities, we have opportunities to work across the multiple intelligences. We also have the opportunity to develop research and recording skills. These skills can foster the learners' development across the curriculum, building independent 'learning how to learn' skills. Above all history can be full of fun and enjoyment – a key motivating factor for all children!

The following mindmap presents the key elements drawn from the Programme of Study for history which should focus our attention on the 'how' of history rather than on the 'what'.

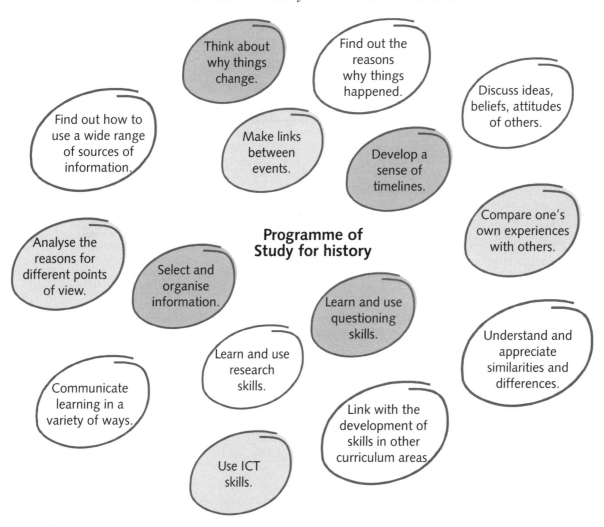

The following range of suggestions taken from the Programme of Study in history present opportunities for the planning of general overview studies together with in-depth studies of particular aspects.

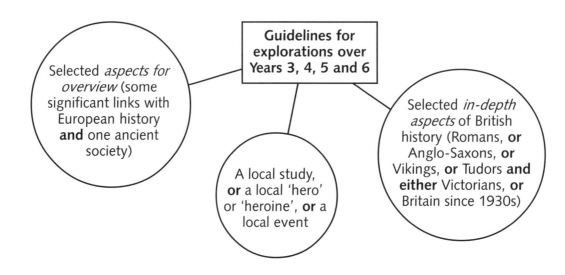

Living history

To mark the 150th anniversary of Barrowby School, the staff and pupils, the church and the community of Barrowby celebrate their Victorian heritage.

Photographer: Kate Waghorn

Head teacher: Sylvia West

Teaching Problem-solving and Thinking Skills through History

TASC: Thinking Actively in a Social Context

BELLE WALLACE

Many aspects of the knowledge, skills and understandings set out in the non-statutory guidelines for personal, social and citizenship education . . . inevitably permeate good history teaching, which involves discussing incomplete sources, comparing accounts and interpretations, rooted in local family history. . . . At Key Stage 2 . . . (learners) should reflect with imagination on social, moral, spiritual and cultural issues, understand other people's experiences and points of view and think about the lives of people living in other places and times, people with different values and customs, considering social and moral dilemmas. What splendid opportunities for creative and lively history!   (Cooper 2000)

The revised National Curriculum Guidelines for the teaching of history (QCA/DfEE 2000) encourage great flexibility of approach in developing history topics both at Key Stage 1 and Key Stage 2. Teachers are urged to progress from focusing on the immediate experiences of the individual to the broader framework of the family; and hence to the wider needs and values of the community. Teachers can work creatively to develop schemes of work from the immediately relevant and concrete experiences of learners and then to progress to deeper, more abstract concepts. This potential for flexibility of depth and breadth of content and approach especially enables teachers to accommodate the more advanced perceptions of able learners.

History presents a wonderful opportunity for cross-curricular explorations such as art, music, literature, science, technology, design, literacy, numeracy, geography. There is plenty of opportunity for development across the range of multiple intelligences; in particular the emotional and social intelligences, which in turn foster and nourish self-esteem and concern for others – a major need in our current society. Working across the multiple intelligences is inevitably linked with accommodating a variety of learning styles – encouraging learners to discover and develop their strengths and preferred ways of learning.

Language undoubtedly is the major tool for communication both for school learning and for lifelong learning. Learning to express oneself and learning to listen to others lie at the roots of democracy: and cooperative discussion in history can provide a major vehicle for sharing ideas, explaining one's point of view, understanding the opposing point of view, and questioning conclusions that were previously closed.

As an essential part of language development, history topics invite questions of What? When? Who? Where? How? – and most importantly **Why?**

There is a great deal of research to show that the 'intelligence' of an individual is not a fixed commodity that can be easily measured and quantified: the intelligent functioning of any individual is capable of change and growth in a climate where problem-solving and thinking skills are systematically taught and rewarded. The teaching of history naturally lends itself to the development of problem-solving and thinking skills in both logical and creative domains. Working with young primary learners, key words – such as: because, so that, although, in order to – are the lynch pins of early logical thinking. At Key Stage 2, the use of these basic thinking words needs to progress into more advanced thinking processes such as: weighing up evidence, prioritising ideas, drawing reasoned conclusions. The development of creative thinking has the seeds of its development in activities which encourage learners to imagine, explore alternatives, find another way or reason. These activities lead the way for learners to confidently ask the key questions of: What would happen if? What might have happened? What could possibly happen?

- The purpose of this chapter (and subsequent chapters) is not to suggest yet another new initiative! This first chapter will present a well-researched framework for the explicit teaching techniques and learning activities which together form the foundation of the development of problem-solving and thinking skills through history. This framework is called TASC: Thinking Actively in a Social Context.

- Subsequent chapters will examine topics from the National Curriculum Programmes of Study and will show how these topics have been developed with an emphasis on promoting problem-solving and thinking skills.

In addition to the two main purposes outlined above, all chapters will demonstrate how history can be used to develop children's strengths across the range of multiple intelligences and learning styles; together with a range of recording and communication skills.

The mindmap overleaf summarises the main strengths of history as a cross-curricular tool for extending teaching skills and enhancing learning skills.

REFLECT

Reflect on the comments made by teachers during staff discussion sessions (pp. 6–7).

- First highlight those issues which are common to your school; then

- Add any other issues which reflect concerns in your school.

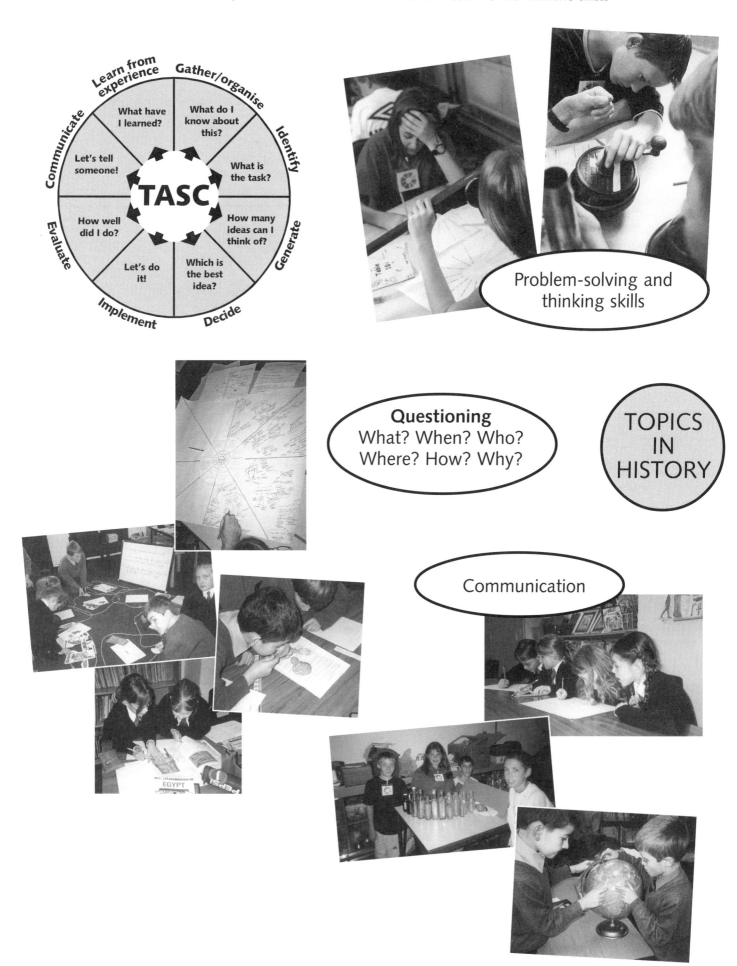

Problem-solving and thinking skills

Questioning
What? When? Who?
Where? How? Why?

TOPICS IN HISTORY

Communication

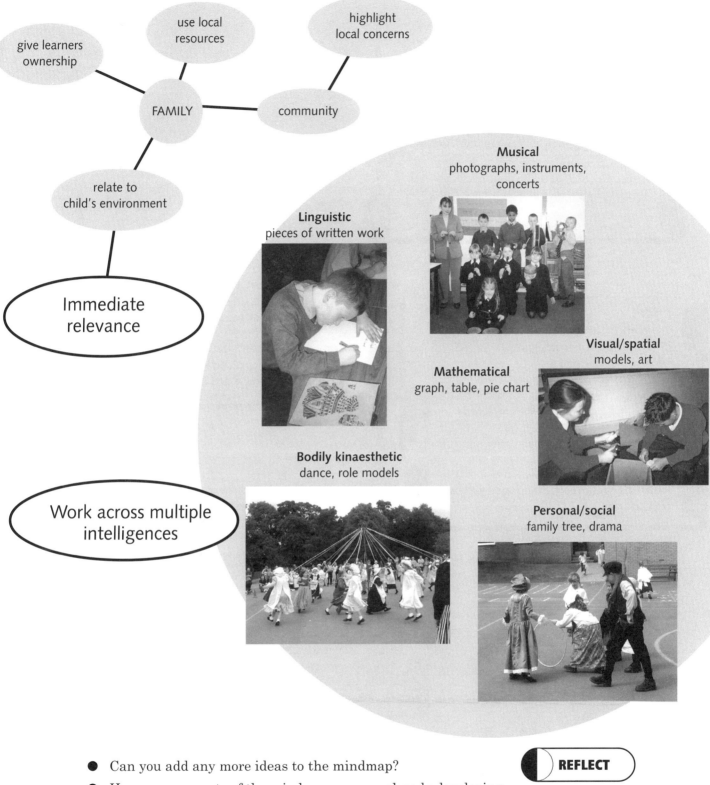

give learners ownership

use local resources

highlight local concerns

FAMILY

community

relate to child's environment

Immediate relevance

Work across multiple intelligences

Musical
photographs, instruments, concerts

Linguistic
pieces of written work

Visual/spatial
models, art

Mathematical
graph, table, pie chart

Bodily kinaesthetic
dance, role models

Personal/social
family tree, drama

REFLECT

- Can you add any more ideas to the mindmap?
- How many aspects of the mindmap are you already developing in history lessons?
- To what extent do you use topics in history as stimuli for other lesson activities?
- Do the children's learning activities in history range across the multiple intelligences and learning styles?
- Do you consciously use history topics to teach problem-solving and thinking skills?
- Do you systematically train communication skills through history lessons?

In our school we have to give so much time to the core subjects of literacy, numeracy and science that we can barely squeeze in the other subjects.

Yes, but perhaps we can look for ways to increase the use of 'content' subjects as a base for learning skills in literacy, numeracy and science.

After all, we need to look for ways to increase the learning of skills across the curriculum.

We are already looking at ways to support the wide range of learning styles in a class.

And there are so many aspects to the learning of history that we can use. A history topic for activities in art, music, drama, model-making, ICT etc.

Yes, accommodating various learning styles and developing children's multiple intelligences are one and the same thing.

We need to look at the range of recording skills that we are focusing on.

Yes, there are skills such as making mindmaps, flow charts, graphs and pie charts that we need to use consistently across the curriculum.

Also, a wide range of researching and communicating skills should develop oral, visual and spatial competencies as well as writing skills.

A major problem is that children generally don't listen and working in groups is problematic.

Also, the attention span of many children is short which makes any independent topic work difficult to handle.

But we need to train the skills of listening and working in groups, and using relevant history topics linked with the children's environment will give us a headstart in this. Children will more readily respond to activities when they are really interested. They need to relate their learning to the reality of their own lives.

Our major problem lies in developing the children's language for learning and we need to focus on this.

We already do, but a vital way to effect this is to develop children's skills in discussion. If learners can't express their ideas orally, how can they express them in written form?

History is the ideal subject for developing discussion techniques. There are so many different interpretations and conclusions that can be drawn, and so many different points of view that can be explored.

Our priority is to raise our children's self-esteem.

Yes, we are already working towards achieving that for all our children. We need to convey the real message that they are capable of learning for themselves – that they are capable of improving.

Setting challenges and problems for them to solve and then teaching them the relevant strategies to use, means that not only will we raise their self-esteem, but we will also equip them with life-skills.

History is full of opportunities for problem-solving and we need to explore how we teach history in the classroom. We need to ask ourselves the following questions: Do we stick to the content as fact gathering? Or do we use the content as a base for setting problems to be solved?

We need to develop good values and attitudes so that we raise the ethos of our school and the community.

Yes, we are already working hard to do that, but by taking topics in history particularly, we can ask children to reflect on causes and consequences of actions in certain social environments. History is about real people making decisions that affect others either for better or for worse.

We can help learners to see and solve problems through the lens of their own experience. The differences caused by race, gender, language, customs and culture are already there in our classrooms and we need to use these as a base for learning.

History is about life and people and about asking questions of why the world is as it is. And what the world might be like in the future – if there is one!

I agree. History is about motives, passions, power, jealousies.

It's also about ordinary people trying to have a decent life – trying to live each day with a modicum of satisfaction and fulfilment.

It's also about leaders and followers – about dominance and subservience – about equality and justice – about generosity and greed. All the big issues of life are there!

History is also great fun! Finding out! Guessing and arguing! Comparing and contrasting! Delving into the past!

Perhaps, most importantly, history is about using problem-solving and thinking skills to reflect on our world and from there to try and make it a better one!

History and problem-solving

There is a history in all men's lives,
Figuring the nature of the times deceased;
The which observed, a man may prophesy,
With a near aim, of the main chance of things
As yet not come to life, which in their seeds
And weak beginnings lie intreasured.
(*Henry IV Part 2*, Act 3 Scene 1, 1.80)

Sometimes people characterize alternatives to traditional approaches to history as throwing open the gates to the barbarians. They fear that where there are multiple 'right' answers, there are no 'wrong' ones, that history becomes a complete fiction or simply a chronological arrangement of ungrounded opinions arrived at by group consensus and used to bolster spurious causes. We take the contrary view, arguing that thinking historically is fundamentally about judgment – about building and evaluating warranted or grounded interpretations. . . . [We need to] help students to learn how to gather and analyze information about the past. (Levstik and Barton 2001)

Being human means thinking and feeling; it means reflecting on the past and visioning into the future. We experience; we give voice to that experience; others reflect on it and give it new form. That new form, in its turn, influences and shapes the way the next generation experience their lives. That is why history matters. (G. Lerner (1997) quoted in Levstik and Barton 2001: 211)

In addition, John H. Arnold suggests the following reasons [for studying history]. Firstly, it is simply enjoyment. 'There is pleasure in studying the past, just as there is in studying music or art or films or botany or the stars. Some of us gain pleasure from looking at old documents, gazing at old paintings and seeing something of the world that is not entirely our own' (Arnold (2000). Secondly, history is a vehicle for developing our thinking inasmuch as it takes us out of our present context and makes us consider how other people behaved thus leading to the mind questioning why and how we do the things we do. Finally, history should make us feel differently about ourselves. History shows that there are many courses of action for us to consider. Arnold concludes that, 'History provides us with the tools to dissent.' Just what the gifted and talented need! (Mordecai 2002: 114)

How do you know who you are unless you know where you've come from? How can you tell what's going to happen unless you know what's happened before? History isn't just about the past. It's why we are who we are – and about what's next. (Tony Robinson (1999) *The National Curriculum Handbook*, quoted in Mordecai 2002: 114)

Theoretical background to the model of problem-solving and thinking skills used throughout this text

Throughout the 1980s, Belle Wallace and Harvey B. Adams were concerned to find a coherent and justifiable framework for the teaching and learning of problem-solving and thinking skills across the curriculum. They wanted to research a framework that would enhance the abilities of *all* learners: providing support and scaffolding for weaker learners, and enabling more able learners to accelerate through basic stages of learning into areas of greater depth and breadth. This research meant finding a sound educational framework for both the teaching methods and the thinking skills that would transfer across the curriculum.

Wallace and Adams surveyed the main thinking skills packages in use around the world. In many cases, they visited the countries and worked with the leaders and researchers in the field of problem-solving and thinking skills. Analysing the results of their research, they assembled the most successful elements of all the projects they had studied and evaluated; and then conducted an intensive ten year action research programme with groups of disadvantaged learners and their teachers.

Strategies and teaching methods were trialled and refined through a cyclical process of action, evaluation, reflection, and modification which involved the students, their teachers, a group of educational psychologists and, of course, the researchers. This process resulted in the active development of a practical model for the teaching of problem-solving and thinking skills known as *TASC: Thinking Actively in a Social Context* (Wallace and Adams 1993) which sets out a framework for the development of a problem-solving and thinking skills approach to the curriculum.

The remainder of this chapter examines:

1. The TASC framework with particular reference to the teaching of history. We will examine the theoretical base, the teaching methodology and a range of core skills and strategies which should be incorporated into any programme purporting to develop a problem-solving and thinking skills approach to the curriculum.

2. How history can involve problem-solving tasks which range across the multiple intelligences and learning styles.

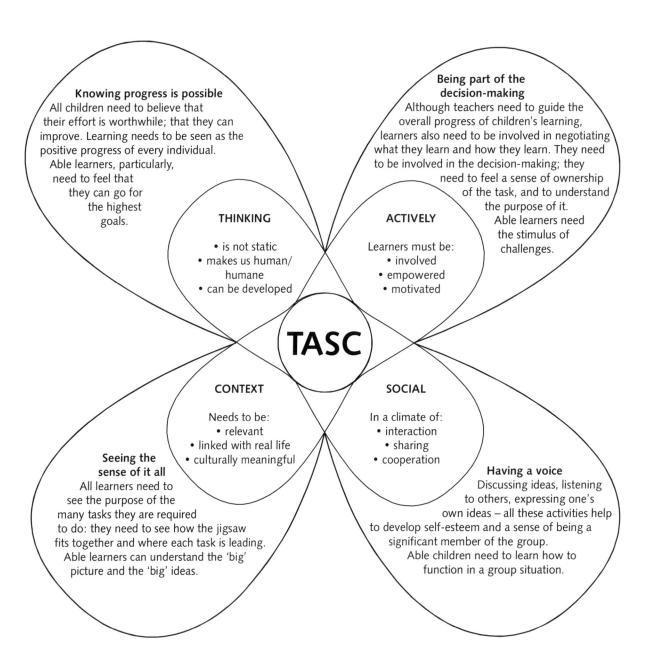

Knowing progress is possible
All children need to believe that
their effort is worthwhile; that they can
improve. Learning needs to be seen as the
positive progress of every individual.
Able learners, particularly,
need to feel that
they can go for
the highest
goals.

**Being part of the
decision-making**
Although teachers need to guide the
overall progress of children's learning,
learners also need to be involved in negotiating
what they learn and how they learn. They need
to be involved in the decision-making; they
need to feel a sense of ownership
of the task, and to understand
the purpose of it.
Able learners need
the stimulus of
challenges.

THINKING

• is not static
• makes us human/
  humane
• can be developed

ACTIVELY

Learners must be:
• involved
• empowered
• motivated

TASC

CONTEXT

Needs to be:
• relevant
• linked with real life
• culturally meaningful

SOCIAL

In a climate of:
• interaction
• sharing
• cooperation

**Seeing the
sense of it all**
All learners need to
see the purpose of the
many tasks they are required
to do: they need to see how the jigsaw
fits together and where each task is leading.
Able learners can understand the 'big'
picture and the 'big' ideas.

Having a voice
Discussing ideas, listening
to others, expressing one's
own ideas – all these activities help
to develop self-esteem and a sense of being a
significant member of the group.
Able children need to learn how to
function in a group situation.

The basic tenets of TASC (extended from Wallace 2001)

REFLECT   Would you like to add any more ideas to the basic tenets of TASC?

Understanding the theory that informs TASC

Good teachers generally have well-developed personal and social intelligences since they can manage a wide range of individuals in a classroom situation with superb skill and understanding. One could argue that teachers who specialise in teaching history are especially strong in these intelligences, since history is essentially about understanding people and their actions. Also, of course, history not only requires the logical skills of analysis, but also the creative skills of imagination which are brought to bear on the study of artefacts, documents, records, illustrations, music, paintings.

Understanding the theory that informs TASC and then putting the theory into practice not only develops pupils' problem-solving skills, but also presents opportunities for working across the range of multiple intelligences. These opportunities are supported by the general aims of history and the skills teachers are endeavouring to develop in their pupils. Undoubtedly, the theory behind TASC will elicit a sure empathetic resonance with what is considered to be good history teaching. However, empathy and intuition, while being extremely powerful diagnostic and teaching tools, need the backing of sound theory and analysis. The TASC framework aims to provide both the analysis of sound theory and the creative application of this theory in teaching methodology and learning activities.

Vygotsky's 'Development of Higher Psychological Processes'

Vygotsky (1978) reveals his perceptive understanding of how we all best learn in his text *Mind in Society*, and he confirms what good teachers have always intuitively known and effectively practised. The role of the teacher is that of the senior learner who helps the apprentice learner transform her or his existing knowledge into deeper, more advanced knowledge. The teacher provides the mental scaffolding for the learner and removes that scaffolding as the learner achieves mastery of concepts, methods and skills. The artistry of the effective teacher lies in the skills of questioning, guiding, probing and prodding the learner through the hazy, uncertain stage of not knowing to the certain awareness of knowing. The aim of teaching should be to guide the learner to independence, to equip the learner with 'learning how to learn' skills so that learning is a lifelong pursuit. How many 'subject' books remain unopened after the learner has left formal schooling? Also, very importantly, the teacher models thinking processes, talks her or his thinking 'out loud', demonstrates the skills of enquiry, the feelings of uncertainty, the investigating eagerness of the search for possible answers. The artistry of teaching lies in the dynamic interaction between mentor and pupil, in the vibrancy of a classroom where the exploration is the key aim and interested fascination the prime motivation.

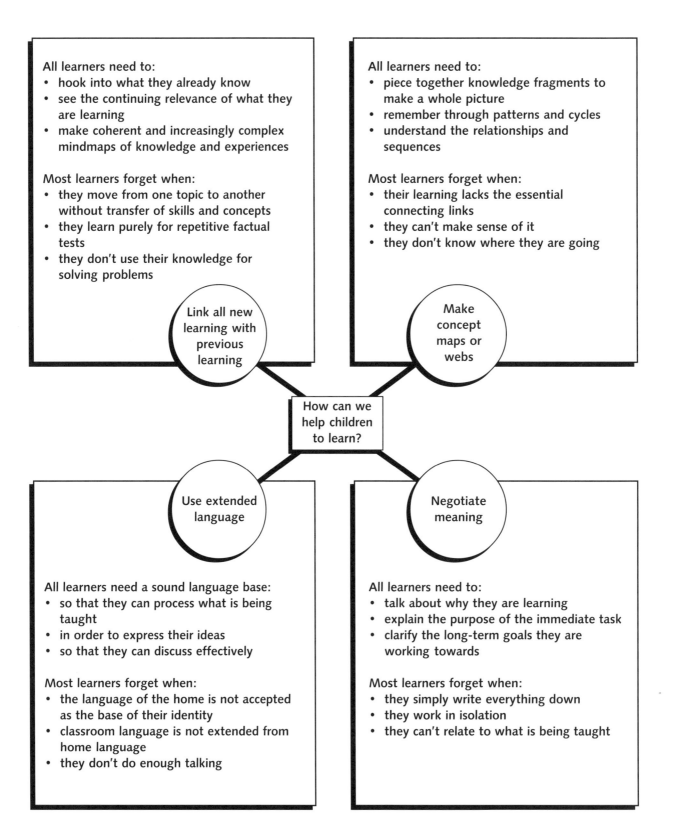

All learners need to:
- hook into what they already know
- see the continuing relevance of what they are learning
- make coherent and increasingly complex mindmaps of knowledge and experiences

Most learners forget when:
- they move from one topic to another without transfer of skills and concepts
- they learn purely for repetitive factual tests
- they don't use their knowledge for solving problems

Link all new learning with previous learning

All learners need to:
- piece together knowledge fragments to make a whole picture
- remember through patterns and cycles
- understand the relationships and sequences

Most learners forget when:
- their learning lacks the essential connecting links
- they can't make sense of it
- they don't know where they are going

Make concept maps or webs

How can we help children to learn?

Use extended language

All learners need a sound language base:
- so that they can process what is being taught
- in order to express their ideas
- so that they can discuss effectively

Most learners forget when:
- the language of the home is not accepted as the base of their identity
- classroom language is not extended from home language
- they don't do enough talking

Negotiate meaning

All learners need to:
- talk about why they are learning
- explain the purpose of the immediate task
- clarify the long-term goals they are working towards

Most learners forget when:
- they simply write everything down
- they work in isolation
- they can't relate to what is being taught

Vygotsky's 'Development of Higher Psychological Processes' (extended from Wallace 2001)

Componential

Develop skills and strategies to plan, monitor, reflect and transfer

* Use everyday experiences within the family and the community as the base for learning
* As relevant skills are used, give them appropriate names
* Deliberately look for ways to use skills systematically across the curriculum
* Take time to discuss the usefulness of the skill and provide opportunities for practice

Activities
* Explore local issues
* Investigate and use local resources
* Interview members of the local community
* Use Venn diagrams, pie charts, graphs to organise ideas
* Construct mindmaps, flow charts to clarify links
* Brainstorm ideas, sort and prioritise them

Experiential

Deal with novelty, autonomise and transfer strategies

* Deliberately ask pupils to recall and use an appropriate skill
* Discuss how and why a learned skill can be used in a new topic
* Talk about the pupils developing a repertoire of thinking tools
* Keep a class log of skills being developed and monitor use

Activities
* What useful skill did we use in a similar investigation?
* Why would it be useful to prioritise ideas at this point?
* Should we conduct another survey?
* Which thinking skill would be appropriate to use here?
* How can we find out this information?

Contextual

Adapt, select and shape real-world environments:

* Use history topics which closely relate to life
* Draw parallels with everyday problems – comparing and contrasting
* Create an atmosphere of learners as active problem-solvers
* Find opportunities for real problem-solving in the school and community

Activities
* Our school has a mixture of cultures. How can we get to understand each other better?
* What suggestions can we make to improve the local museum?
* In what ways was the Victorian community similar/different from ours?
* What benefits of the Roman occupation can we still see in Britain?

**Sternberg's 'Triarchic Theory of Intellectual Development'
(extended from Wallace 2001)**

Sternberg's 'Triarchic Theory of Intellectual Development'

Actively developing intelligence

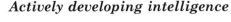

Robert Sternberg (1985) has led the way in producing evidence to show that our 'intelligence' is not a fixed, unchanging commodity that can be measured. Although our inherited characteristics vary, we can all be taught a range of thinking and problem-solving skills which will enhance both our cognitive and our emotional performances. Sternberg argues that 'intelligence' is the capacity to see and solve problems and these problems need first to be embedded in real-life scenarios, with an accompanying range of thinking strategies which are regularly used and trained until they form an automatic repertoire we can call upon. We can all be taught how to plan and monitor our thinking: we can be taught how to reflect on our performance and then to revise and improve our behaviour. We are modifiable as human beings! However, we need to be taught in a problem-solving way and to have role models who demonstrate the thinking strategies we need to acquire. Hence the role of a teacher should be that of a senior problem-solver, taking the role of investigator with the learners: not the role of dispenser of knowledge about a topic.

REFLECT

- How did you acquire your love for and understanding of history?

- Why do certain periods in history fascinate you?

- What fuels your continuing interest in history?

- What were the qualities of your most outstanding history teacher?

Considering the broad teaching principles which underpin TASC

COMMENT

The broad teaching principles of TASC have evolved through:

- The worldwide research that was initially conducted on the teaching principles which underpin successful problem-solving and thinking skills programmes.

- The intensive action research programme over ten years which trialled, evaluated and refined a range of the most effective teaching and learning strategies.

- The ongoing classroom research into teacher and learner interaction which raises the levels of all children's performance, and hence whole school development.

The diagram opposite summarises the key characteristics of the TASC problem-solving and thinking skills teaching and learning methodology. The diagram is focused particularly on the teaching of history.

Reflect on the broad teaching strategies you use in the classroom

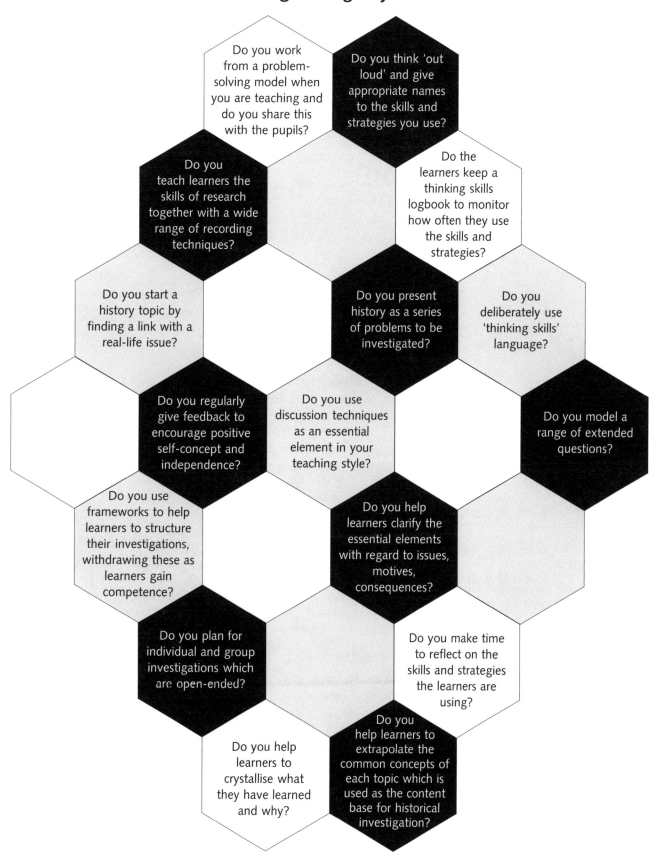

Do you work from a problem-solving model when you are teaching and do you share this with the pupils?

Do you think 'out loud' and give appropriate names to the skills and strategies you use?

Do you teach learners the skills of research together with a wide range of recording techniques?

Do the learners keep a thinking skills logbook to monitor how often they use the skills and strategies?

Do you start a history topic by finding a link with a real-life issue?

Do you present history as a series of problems to be investigated?

Do you deliberately use 'thinking skills' language?

Do you regularly give feedback to encourage positive self-concept and independence?

Do you use discussion techniques as an essential element in your teaching style?

Do you model a range of extended questions?

Do you use frameworks to help learners to structure their investigations, withdrawing these as learners gain competence?

Do you help learners clarify the essential elements with regard to issues, motives, consequences?

Do you plan for individual and group investigations which are open-ended?

Do you make time to reflect on the skills and strategies the learners are using?

Do you help learners to crystallise what they have learned and why?

Do you help learners to extrapolate the common concepts of each topic which is used as the content base for historical investigation?

Use the diagram to reflect on your teaching methodology.　　　　　(**REFLECT**

The basic TASC Problem-solving Wheel

Pupils can cut out and laminate the TASC Problem-solving Wheel then fasten it with paper fasteners into their exercise book or thinking skills logbook. The pupils can also re-design the Wheel and invent their own symbols for each stage of problem-solving. The pupils can then use the Wheels to guide their thinking and planning. In addition, the Wheel can be enlarged on to A3 sheets and the pupils can write out their thinking and planning in detail. (See the pupils' planning on p. 106).

Questions to develop thinking in the TASC Problem-solving Framework

Many learners have not developed a repertoire of relevant questions to stimulate their thinking processes, nor have they an adequate command of thinking language to express their ideas. It is important that teachers consistently model a range of appropriate thinking language and the TASC Questioning Wheel provides starting points for this. The children need to have copies of this Questioning Wheel and then they can refer to it whenever they are working on a problem-solving project.

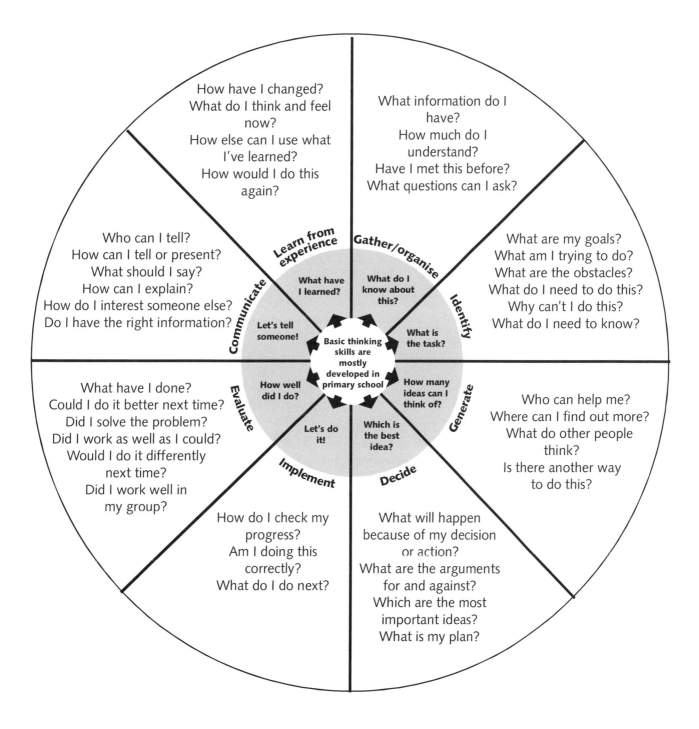

The extended TASC Problem-solving Framework

- Develops metacognition
- Affirms learning is growth
- Gives opportunity to transfer skills and knowledge
- Crystallises what has been learned
- Gives verbal labels to skills learned
- Builds autonomy in learning
- Develops self-confidence and self-esteem

- Reflect on the whole thinking process
- Compare with previous performance
- Look for uses in other lessons
- Refer back to original knowledge mindmap
- Discuss what has been learned
- Name the skills used

- Develops a real purpose for the task
- Encourages self-confidence
- Develops personal strengths
- Develops a repertoire of skills
- Encourages social interaction

- Create a 'real' audience
- Develop a sharing classroom
- Make real use of learners' work
- Celebrate strengths of multiple intelligences
- Make use of different learning styles
- Encourage communication

Learn from experience

What have I learned?

Communicate

Let's tell someone!

How well did I do?

Evaluate

Let's do it!

TA

- Check with learners if goal was achieved
- Refer back to original ideas and planning
- Think about ways to improve next time
- Give opportunity to improve
- Discuss how well the groups cooperated

Implement

- Builds the climate for learning how to learn
- Encourages self-assessment
- Discourages 'first time perfect' thinking
- Accepts mistakes as part of learning

- Use a wide range of activities
- Teach a range of recording techniques
- Develop research skills
- Demonstrate new procedures

- Develops multiple intelligences/learning styles
- Encourages creativity
- Discourages 'one right way' thinking
- Promotes differentiation

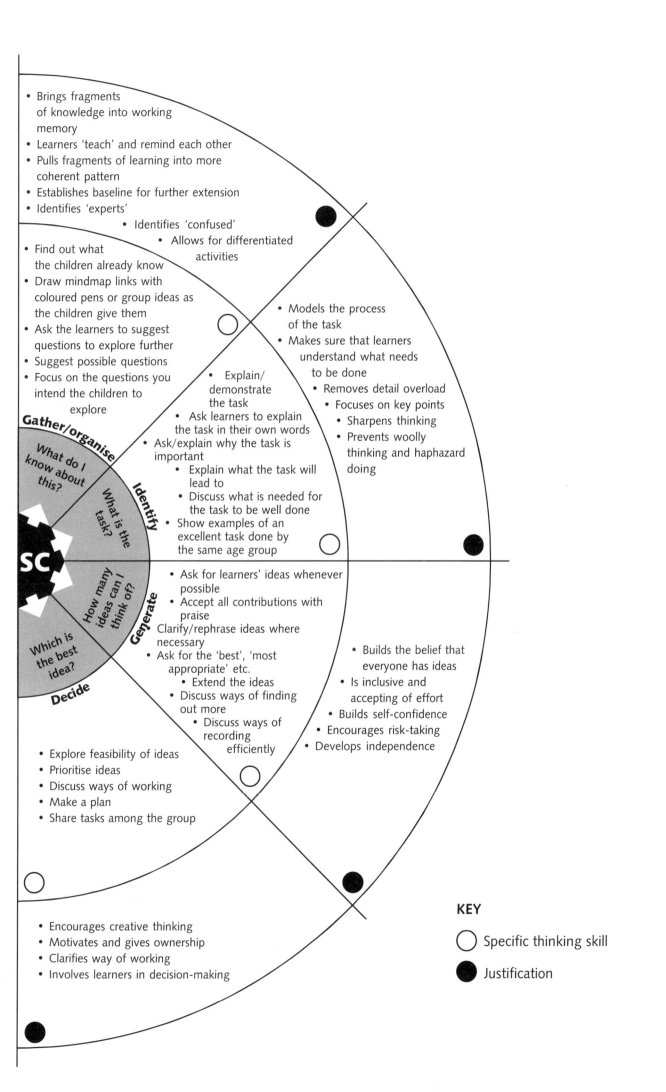

- Brings fragments of knowledge into working memory
- Learners 'teach' and remind each other
- Pulls fragments of learning into more coherent pattern
- Establishes baseline for further extension
- Identifies 'experts'
- Identifies 'confused'
- Allows for differentiated activities

- Find out what the children already know
- Draw mindmap links with coloured pens or group ideas as the children give them
- Ask the learners to suggest questions to explore further
- Suggest possible questions
- Focus on the questions you intend the children to explore

Gather/organise

What do I know about this?

What is the task?

Identify

SC

How many ideas can I think of?

Generate

Which is the best idea?

Decide

- Explain/demonstrate the task
- Ask learners to explain the task in their own words
- Ask/explain why the task is important
- Explain what the task will lead to
- Discuss what is needed for the task to be well done
- Show examples of an excellent task done by the same age group

- Models the process of the task
- Makes sure that learners understand what needs to be done
- Removes detail overload
- Focuses on key points
- Sharpens thinking
- Prevents woolly thinking and haphazard doing

- Ask for learners' ideas whenever possible
- Accept all contributions with praise
- Clarify/rephrase ideas where necessary
- Ask for the 'best', 'most appropriate' etc.
- Extend the ideas
- Discuss ways of finding out more
- Discuss ways of recording efficiently

- Builds the belief that everyone has ideas
- Is inclusive and accepting of effort
- Builds self-confidence
- Encourages risk-taking
- Develops independence

- Explore feasibility of ideas
- Prioritise ideas
- Discuss ways of working
- Make a plan
- Share tasks among the group

- Encourages creative thinking
- Motivates and gives ownership
- Clarifies way of working
- Involves learners in decision-making

KEY

◯ Specific thinking skill

● Justification

Extending the TASC Framework into a menu of strategies for classroom interaction in history

Study the extended TASC Problem-solving Framework (pp. 18–19). Use it to plan the range of teaching and learning strategies you are using in your classroom.

While all the stages of the TASC Problem-solving Wheel are important, there are four critical stages which should be present in any programme purporting to develop thinking skills.

- **Gather and organise**   This stage is important because all learners have fragments of knowledge which need to be organised into a coherent pattern which links them all together. In addition, learners need to bring what they already know into their working memory ready for repair, extension and action. Many learners, especially able learners, repeat what they already know several times as they move to different key stages. This assessment of prior learning need not always be an oral exercise: it is equally valuable to give the children a list of key questions around a topic and if they already know the basic work then they can move on to extension activities. The important point is that teachers must plan extension opportunities for those learners who demonstrate the need.

- **Identify**   Many learners lose sight of the task they are undertaking as they get bogged down in detail or in producing an 'attractive' product. Very able learners can get lost in the complexity of the task because they see the deeper implications or consequences. Keeping a laser look at the purpose of the task is vital for the focusing of attention and mental energy. Also, keeping the purpose of the task in the forefront of thinking helps with evaluating the success of it.

- **Evaluate**   Learners need to be trained to evaluate their work – the skill doesn't just happen! Learners need to see examples of 'good' and 'excellent' work and to discuss why the work has merit. They need to tease out the criteria for excellence and then work towards replicating those qualities. In addition, very able learners so easily accomplish the tasks set to an 'acceptable standard' that they need clear constructive guidance on how to improve their performance. Plans and drafts need to be kept and displayed alongside the finished work. This conveys the message that good work is not a 'one-off' attempt, and it also shows other children the processes of development towards the finished work.

- **Learn from experience**   This is the key learning point! Unless learners reflect on the learning process, they will seldom, if ever, crystallise what has been learned; how they learned; and what skills and knowledge they have mastered. This is the essential stage for retaining and transferring what has been learned: yet it is the stage which is most commonly left out. Although time is at a premium in a busy school day, the time spent in reflecting on and consolidating what has been learned will save time in the long term and will enable all learners to feel a sense of progress and satisfaction.

Developing Tools for Effective Thinking which feed into the TASC Problem-solving Wheel

In developing TASC, learners and teachers identified the Tools for Effective Thinking that they used most often in the early stages of building the learners' repertoire of thinking skills. These core skills are summarised overleaf (p. 22).

Think about the core of effective thinking tools outlined on p. 22:

- Which thinking tools do you use most often?

- Do you give names to these tools as you use them?

- Can you add any more to your teaching repertoire?

Extending the TASC Tools for Effective Thinking

There are many action words that can be called thinking tools. Some of these are subject specific while others are generic and should be consciously used across the curriculum. The mindmap on p. 23 extends the basic core of Tools for Effective Thinking. The mindmap is useful as a checklist when planning classroom activities. Most of the tools are both necessary and suitable for all learners although the language could be adjusted to suit the level of understanding of different groups of learners.

Most commonly used TASC Tools for Effective Thinking

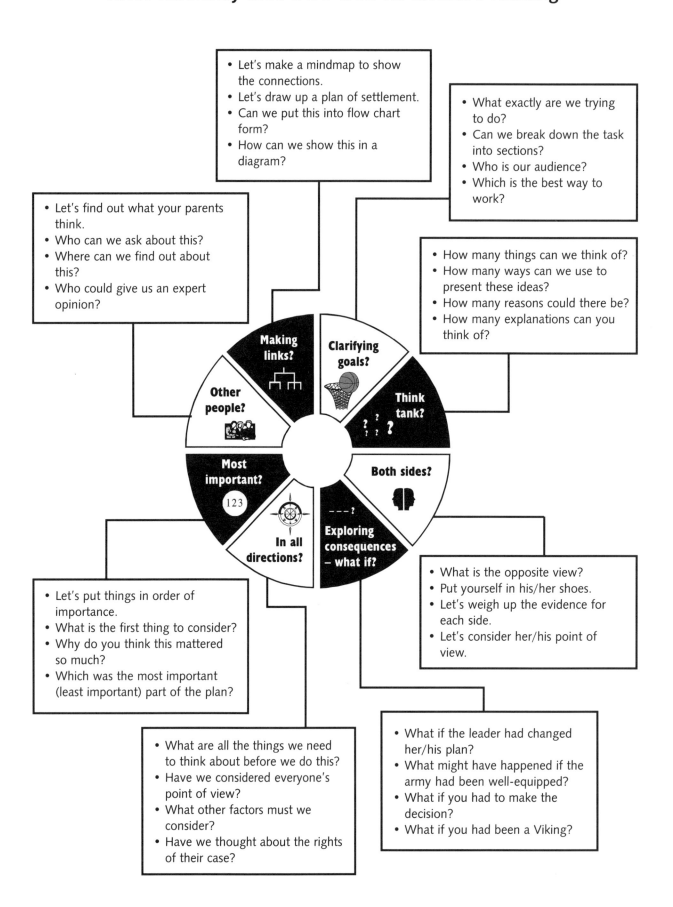

- Let's make a mindmap to show the connections.
- Let's draw up a plan of settlement.
- Can we put this into flow chart form?
- How can we show this in a diagram?

- What exactly are we trying to do?
- Can we break down the task into sections?
- Who is our audience?
- Which is the best way to work?

- Let's find out what your parents think.
- Who can we ask about this?
- Where can we find out about this?
- Who could give us an expert opinion?

- How many things can we think of?
- How many ways can we use to present these ideas?
- How many reasons could there be?
- How many explanations can you think of?

Making links?

Clarifying goals?

Other people?

Think tank?

Most important?

Both sides?

In all directions?

Exploring consequences – what if?

- Let's put things in order of importance.
- What is the first thing to consider?
- Why do you think this mattered so much?
- Which was the most important (least important) part of the plan?

- What is the opposite view?
- Put yourself in his/her shoes.
- Let's weigh up the evidence for each side.
- Let's consider her/his point of view.

- What are all the things we need to think about before we do this?
- Have we considered everyone's point of view?
- What other factors must we consider?
- Have we thought about the rights of their case?

- What if the leader had changed her/his plan?
- What might have happened if the army had been well-equipped?
- What if you had to make the decision?
- What if you had been a Viking?

Extending the TASC Tools for Effective Thinking

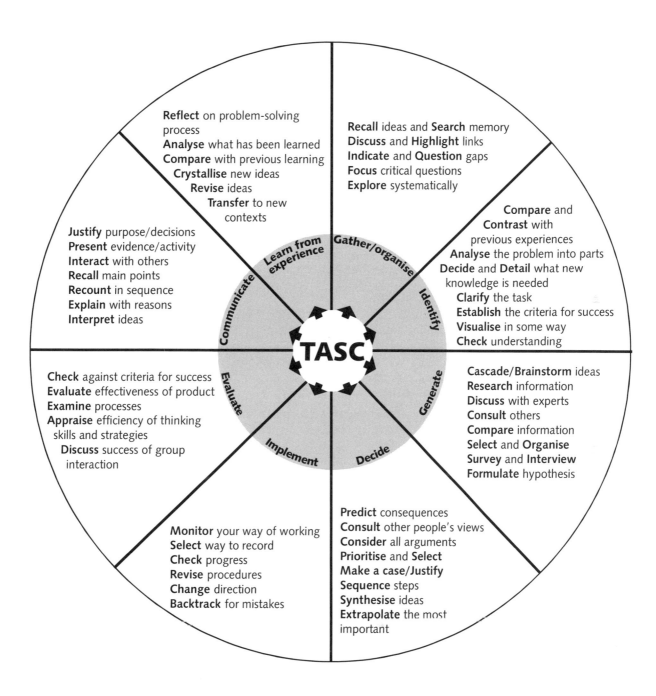

Extending the TASC Problem-solving Wheel across the multiple intelligences

All the stages of the TASC Wheel can be used to develop a wide range of research skills such as surveys, questionnaires, interview techniques, internet skills; as well as recording skills such as mindmaps, flow charts, star charts, spidergrams, graphs, Venn diagrams, information and communication technology (ICT) etc.

The TASC Problem-solving Wheel and the Tools for Effective Thinking also extend quite naturally to accommodate the full range of learning styles across the multiple intelligences. The problem-solving stages of 'Decide', 'Implement' and 'Communicate' are particularly open to interpretation through activities in linguistic, logical/mathematical, visual/spatial, musical, bodily kinesthetic, interpersonal and intrapersonal intelligences. (This text subsumes Gardner's (1990) suggestion of a naturalist intelligence as being contained within the original suggestion of seven.)

It should be stated, however, that while everyone has a full range of abilities across the multiple intelligences, we all have some abilities which are more dominant that others: and children need to have some choice of activities, sometimes working in their dominant intelligence(s), sometimes exploring opportunities through their less dominant intelligence(s), or indeed, sometimes using a combination.

The chart opposite details the range of possible activities across the multiple intelligences. Obviously, some activities incorporate several intelligences or can be focused mainly within one intelligence.

REFLECT

Take some time to do a reflective audit on the range of activities you use in history. Do you create opportunities for learners to work across the multiple intelligences?

Extending the menu of possible activities even further to include a range of higher order thinking skills

Earlier in this chapter, we have considered a universally generated and extensively trialled problem-solving model known as TASC which learners can use to practise a repertoire of thinking skills. We have also considered extending this problem-solving model across the multiple intelligences. However, there is another layer of thinking which extends the menu of teaching and learning activities even further, and that is to consider activities from the perspective of a range of higher order thinking skills. These higher order thinking skills are embedded in the extended TASC model but it is useful to look at them from a separate perspective.

Activities to extend the TASC Problem-solving Wheel across the multiple intelligences

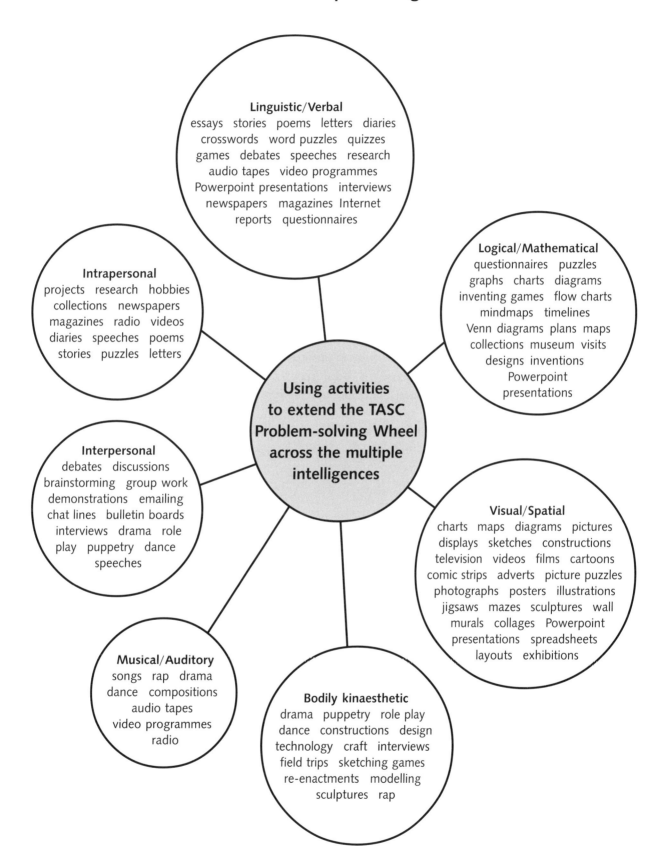

Benjamin Bloom is usually quoted in connection with a taxonomy of higher order thinking skills, but his work has been superceded in the light of what we now know about how children learn. Children do not progress upwards in separate and disparate stages from acquiring and understanding knowledge through analysing, creating and evaluating knowledge: rather they move backwards and forwards through the different kinds of thinking as the task demands. All children do this. The factor which varies is *the level of complexity of the task*. Young children and children of average ability are capable of functioning in all the layers of the so called 'higher order thinking skills' if the content and demand of the task is appropriate. Very able children are capable of dealing with greater complexity of content and task: they are capable of greater depth and breadth of reasoning.

The highest level of thinking occurs when learners (including adults) bring all their thinking skills together in the process of problem-solving. These problems relate to life in general as well as to subjects in the school curriculum. Hence when we are discussing 'higher order thinking skills' we could say that, firstly, learners need to acquire knowledge in as many ways as is possible – from life experience, from a variety of activities and resources, from other people: and then to demonstrate in some way that they understand the knowledge. We could argue that these two cognitive and emotional activities form the base of what we know. Thereafter, learners need to have experience in making the links between the 'bits' of knowledge; making judgements and decisions; creating something new and pulling all that learning experience into a problem-solving activity.

A menu of activities for projects based on a study of ancient Egypt

Some of these activities are developed in detail Chapter 2. There would not be time to use all the activities, but the 'menu' is prepared so that teachers and pupils can make choices according to both the time available and the pupils' learning strengths. For very able children, an extended project allows them to work in greater depth and breadth, avoiding the repetition of basic knowledge which they have already acquired.

A menu of activities for projects based on a study of ancient Egypt

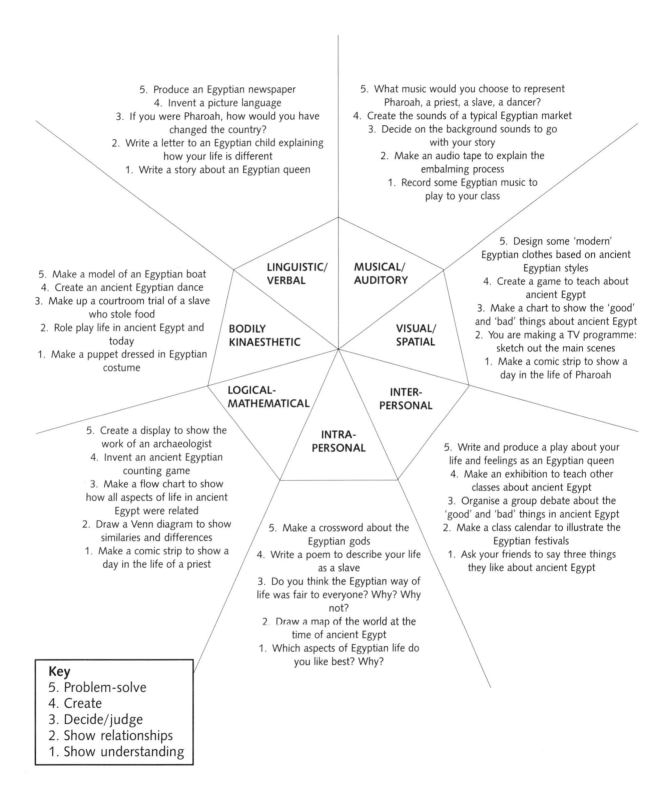

5. Produce an Egyptian newspaper
4. Invent a picture language
3. If you were Pharoah, how would you have changed the country?
2. Write a letter to an Egyptian child explaining how your life is different
1. Write a story about an Egyptian queen

5. What music would you choose to represent Pharoah, a priest, a slave, a dancer?
4. Create the sounds of a typical Egyptian market
3. Decide on the background sounds to go with your story
2. Make an audio tape to explain the embalming process
1. Record some Egyptian music to play to your class

5. Design some 'modern' Egyptian clothes based on ancient Egyptian styles
4. Create a game to teach about ancient Egypt
3. Make a chart to show the 'good' and 'bad' things about ancient Egypt
2. You are making a TV programme: sketch out the main scenes
1. Make a comic strip to show a day in the life of Pharoah

5. Make a model of an Egyptian boat
4. Create an ancient Egyptian dance
3. Make up a courtroom trial of a slave who stole food
2. Role play life in ancient Egypt and today
1. Make a puppet dressed in Egyptian costume

LINGUISTIC/ VERBAL

MUSICAL/ AUDITORY

BODILY KINAESTHETIC

VISUAL/ SPATIAL

LOGICAL- MATHEMATICAL

INTER- PERSONAL

INTRA- PERSONAL

5. Create a display to show the work of an archaeologist
4. Invent an ancient Egyptian counting game
3. Make a flow chart to show how all aspects of life in ancient Egypt were related
2. Draw a Venn diagram to show similarities and differences
1. Make a comic strip to show a day in the life of a priest

5. Write and produce a play about your life and feelings as an Egyptian queen
4. Make an exhibition to teach other classes about ancient Egypt
3. Organise a group debate about the 'good' and 'bad' things in ancient Egypt
2. Make a class calendar to illustrate the Egyptian festivals
1. Ask your friends to say three things they like about ancient Egypt

5. Make a crossword about the Egyptian gods
4. Write a poem to describe your life as a slave
3. Do you think the Egyptian way of life was fair to everyone? Why? Why not?
2. Draw a map of the world at the time of ancient Egypt
1. Which aspects of Egyptian life do you like best? Why?

Key
5. Problem-solve
4. Create
3. Decide/judge
2. Show relationships
1. Show understanding

A menu of activities in history using higher order thinking skills across the multiple intelligences

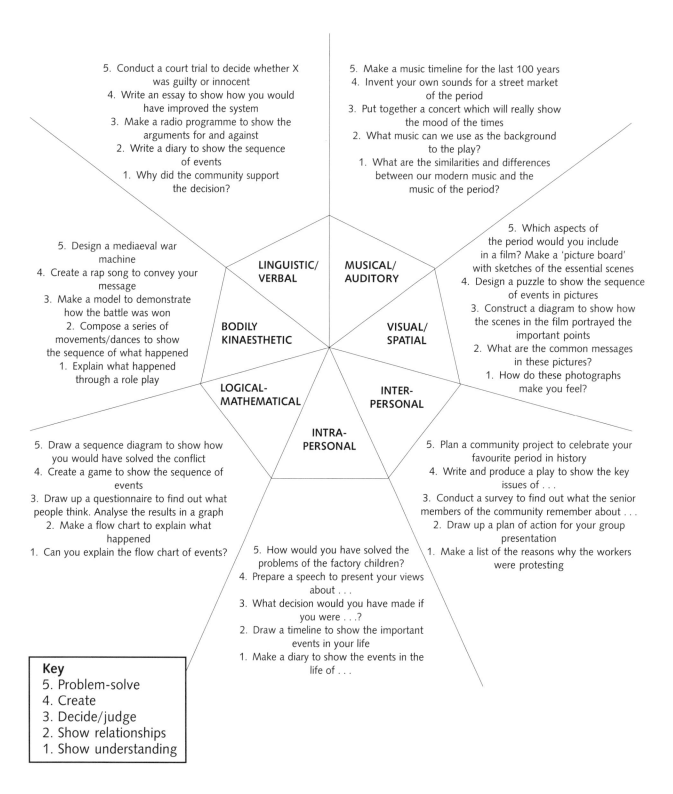

5. Conduct a court trial to decide whether X was guilty or innocent
4. Write an essay to show how you would have improved the system
3. Make a radio programme to show the arguments for and against
2. Write a diary to show the sequence of events
1. Why did the community support the decision?

5. Make a music timeline for the last 100 years
4. Invent your own sounds for a street market of the period
3. Put together a concert which will really show the mood of the times
2. What music can we use as the background to the play?
1. What are the similarities and differences between our modern music and the music of the period?

5. Design a mediaeval war machine
4. Create a rap song to convey your message
3. Make a model to demonstrate how the battle was won
2. Compose a series of movements/dances to show the sequence of what happened
1. Explain what happened through a role play

5. Which aspects of the period would you include in a film? Make a 'picture board' with sketches of the essential scenes
4. Design a puzzle to show the sequence of events in pictures
3. Construct a diagram to show how the scenes in the film portrayed the important points
2. What are the common messages in these pictures?
1. How do these photographs make you feel?

LINGUISTIC/ VERBAL

MUSICAL/ AUDITORY

BODILY KINAESTHETIC

VISUAL/ SPATIAL

LOGICAL- MATHEMATICAL

INTER- PERSONAL

INTRA- PERSONAL

5. Draw a sequence diagram to show how you would have solved the conflict
4. Create a game to show the sequence of events
3. Draw up a questionnaire to find out what people think. Analyse the results in a graph
2. Make a flow chart to explain what happened
1. Can you explain the flow chart of events?

5. Plan a community project to celebrate your favourite period in history
4. Write and produce a play to show the key issues of . . .
3. Conduct a survey to find out what the senior members of the community remember about . . .
2. Draw up a plan of action for your group presentation
1. Make a list of the reasons why the workers were protesting

5. How would you have solved the problems of the factory children?
4. Prepare a speech to present your views about . . .
3. What decision would you have made if you were . . .?
2. Draw a timeline to show the important events in your life
1. Make a diary to show the events in the life of . . .

Key
5. Problem-solve
4. Create
3. Decide/judge
2. Show relationships
1. Show understanding

Conclusion: Why TASC?

The study of history presents ideal opportunities for active problem-solving: and in today's complex society there is an increasing need for learners to be motivated and confident problem-solvers. Perhaps, when we consider all the curriculum subjects, history has the greatest potential to develop the emotional and social intelligences: the intelligence we need to understand the self and the intelligence we need to understand others. The following mindmap shows the potential power of good history teaching when the focus is on self-empowerment.

Using history as a vehicle for self-empowerment

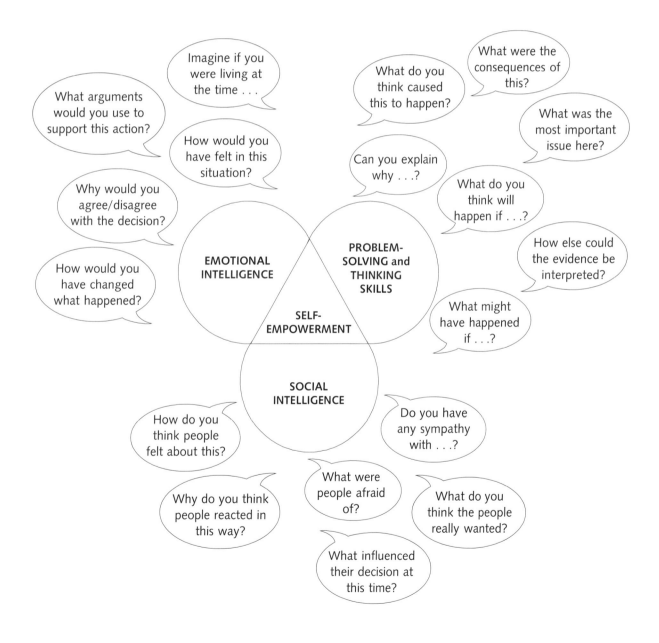

The National Curriculum guidelines for the teaching of history (QCA/ DfEE 2000) encourage and allow teachers the freedom and creativity to work in a problem-solving paradigm across the range of multiple intelligences and learning styles. What a wonderful opportunity for active and creative learning experiences!

In the following chapters:

● Diana Cave (Chapter 2) outlines in depth a project on ancient Egypt which integrates the full TASC Problem-solving Framework, a wide range of Tools for Effective Thinking and activities which cater for learning across the multiple intelligences. This provides a practical model which can be used as a base for a range of other history topics. In addition, Diana includes her planning sheets and samples of work generated by the children.

● Joy Bentley (Chapter 3) presents a TASC teaching/learning model for the use of artefacts as a stimulus for historical investigation. Joy shows how everyday items can be used creatively to stimulate problem-solving and thinking skills.

● In Chapter 4, Tricia McLean, Richard Scott, Selecia Chapman and Sheila Woodhead describe a series of projects in which they have used the TASC Framework to develop pupils' skills in problem-solving.

References and further reading

Arnold, J. H. (2000) *History: A Very Short Introduction*. Oxford: Oxford University Press.

Cooper, H. (2000) *The Teaching of History in Primary Schools*. London: David Fulton Publishers.

Eyre, D. (1999) *Able Children in Ordinary Schools*. London: David Fulton Publishers.

Gardner, H. (1983) *Frames of Mind: The theory of multiple intelligences*, 2nd edn. New York: Basic Books.

Levstik, L. S. and Barton, K. C. (2001) *Doing History: Investigating with children in elementary and middle schools*. NJ: Lawrence Erlbaum Associates.

Mordecai, S. (2002) 'History', in Eyre, D. and Lowe, H. (eds) *Curriculum Provision for the Gifted and Talented in Secondary Schools*, 113–27. London: David Fulton Publishers.

NACE/DfEE Project (1996) *Supporting the Education of Able Children in Maintained Schools*. Oxford: NACE.

Qualifications and Curriculum Authority (QCA)/Department for Education and Employment (DfEE) (2000) *Update of History Schemes of Work*. London: QCA.

Sternberg, R. J. (1985) *Beyond IQ: A triarchic theory of human intelligence*. Cambridge: Cambridge University Press.

Sternberg, R. J. and Davidson, J. E. (eds) (1986) *Conceptions of Giftedness*. Cambridge: Cambridge University Press.

Vygotsky, L. S. (1978) *Mind in Society: The development of higher psychological processes*. Cambridge, MA: Harvard University Press.

Wallace, B. (2000) *Teaching the Very Able Child: Developing a policy and adopting strategies for provision*. London: David Fulton Publishers.

Wallace, B. (ed.) (2001) *Teaching Thinking Skills Across the Primary Curricu-*

lum: A practical approach for all abilities. London: David Fulton Publishers in association with NACE.

Wallace, B. (ed.) (2002) *Teaching Thinking Skills Across the Early Years: A practical approach for children aged 4–7.* London: David Fulton Publishers in association with NACE.

Wallace, B. and Adams, H. B. (1993) *TASC: Thinking Actively in a Social Context.* Oxford: AB Academic Publishers.

Wallace, B. and Bentley, R. (eds) (2001) *Teaching Thinking Skills Across the Middle Years: A practical approach for children aged 9–14.* London: David Fulton Publishers in association with NACE.

Developing TASC Problem-solving and Thinking Skills through a Study of World History: Ancient Egypt

DIANA CAVE

PURPOSE

Our aim was to develop problem-solving and thinking skills in a world history study for Year 4 children using the TASC paradigm and the QCA Ancient Egypt unit of study (QCA/DfEE 2000). In this unit, pupils find out about the way of life of people living in ancient Egypt from archaeological discoveries. They develop their understanding of characteristic features of a society; identify the different ways the past is represented; and use sources of information to make simple observations, inferences and deductions.

Background information

Our school has 480 Key Stage 2 children grouped into 16 mixed ability classes, four classes per year group. Each year group is divided into four ability sets for English and mathematics. Science and non-core foundation subjects are separately planned and timetabled with some cross-curricular links.

The children have experience of the TASC approach, (Wallace 2001) but have not previously been systematically introduced to the TASC Tools for Effective Thinking. Also we wanted to address the need to organise learning activities across the multiple intelligences.

The study of ancient Egypt was timetabled to cover full afternoon blocks over the course of half a term, with some additional work being undertaken in English lessons.

The following outlines of lesson plans (Units 1 to 7) provide guidelines for the activities which were developed. These lesson plans and the activities are explained in detail in the rest of the chapter together with teaching points and examples of the children's work.

Preparation for a TASC study

Learning objective

To revise the individual sections of the TASC Wheel

In preparation for the problem-solving, thinking skills approach to history lessons, a review of the TASC Wheel was carried out in an English lesson. This was part of a study of non-fiction reading comprehension and writing composition from the Text level work of the National Literacy Strategy Year 4 Term 2.

We began by brainstorming as many of the TASC ideas and terminology as we could recall. Collectively, with a little prompting, we assembled a complete TASC Wheel on a display board. In order to refresh the children's working knowledge of the TASC Wheel we set about exploring each segment.

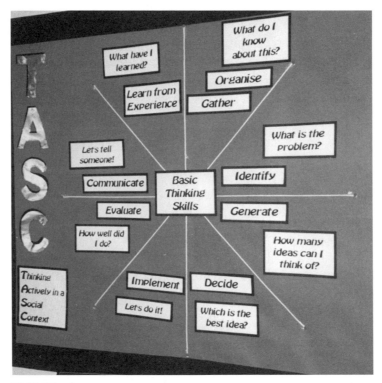

TASC Wheel

Lesson plan Unit 1 (2 hours)

Date:	Curriculum area: History	Cross-curricular/ PSHE links

| POS
1a, 1b, 2, 4, 5 | Learning objective:
• to locate ancient Egypt in time and place | *English*
En1 1b, 1e, 2b,
        2e, 3a, 4c
En2 3a |

Introduction

Class discussion: What do we already know about ancient Egypt? Brainstorm ideas.
Demonstrate how to *gather and organise* the information using a mindmap, grouping existing knowledge under headings, e.g. daily life, houses, death.

Activity

Identify: What is the task?
Share and discuss the learning objective – to locate Egypt in time and place.
Locate Egypt on a globe, in atlases and on photocopied world maps.
Share and discuss a variety of photographs showing Egypt as it is today.
Discuss the natural defences of Egypt – Eastern and Western Deserts and the marshy Nile delta.
On a map of Egypt locate, mark and discuss Nile, pyramids of Giza, Valley of the Kings, deserts, Memphis (capital of Lower Egypt), Thebes (capital of Upper Egypt), Nubia.
Discuss transfer of power from Lower Egypt to Upper Egypt.

Generate: How many ideas can I think of?
Discuss when the children think the ancient Egyptians lived.
Discuss terms AD and BC and biblical references to Egypt – Moses; Flight into Egypt.
Practise counting forwards and backwards across zero.
Introduce a collection of reference materials relating to ancient Egypt.

Decide: Which is the best idea?
Scan texts for information relating to dates.
Note major dates and events on separate Post-it notes.
Arrange these Post-it notes into chronological order.
Calculate time span, to the nearest 1,000 years.

Implement: Let's do it!
Produce a timeline divided into five millennia with one metre representing 1,000 years.
Ask the children to research some key events for the period 0 – present day.
Order a collection of illustrations, marking major events.
Mark on the present day, and a few key events of modern times.
Mark on the discovery of Tutankhamun's tomb in 1922.

Evaluate: How well did I do?
Examine the completed timeline and consider the parts played by individual children.

Plenary

Communicate: Let's tell someone!
Arrange for the timeline to be presented later to another class with a commentary by the children.

Learn from experience: What have I learned?
Reflect upon the knowledge gained about the location of ancient Egypt in time and place.

Notes/implications for future planning

PSHE
1a, 2a, 2c, 2k, 4b

Geography
1a, 2a, 2c, 2d, 3a, 3c, 4a

Mathematics
Ma2 1a, 2a
Ma3 1a, 4a, 4b

Vocabulary
Egypt, Africa, continent, country, city, Cairo, Nile, desert, fertile, defences, BC, AD, timeline, past, present, future, represents

Differentiation
Extensive use of reference materials including CD-ROMs.

Support
Working with a supportive partner, extra input from the teacher.

Resources
Globe
Atlases
Photocopied maps
Photographs of Egypt
Reference materials
Post-it notes
Paper/string and illustrations for the timeline.

Key assessment
Can locate ancient Egypt in time and place.

Lesson plan Unit 2 (3 hours)

Date:	Curriculum area: History	Cross-curricular/ PSHE links

POS
1a, 1b, 2c, 3, 4, 5

Learning objectives:
- to find out about the past from a range of sources of information
- to ask and answer questions about the past

Introduction

Gather/organise: What do I already know about this?
Locate Tutankhamun's burial and discovery on the timeline. How do we find out about the past? Explore the ancient Egypt artefacts box (on loan from the local museum). Discuss the work of archaeologists.
Shared reading: The story of Howard Carter's discovery of the tomb of Tutankhamun in 1922.
(*The Tomb of Tutankhamun*, James Mason, 1991, ISBN 0-582-06816-9)
Examine photocopied diary entries relating to the discovery.
Use a tape recorder to record the 'hot seating' of a variety of characters – Howard Carter, Lord Caernarvon, Egyptian workers, water boy.

Activity

Identify: What is the task?
Discuss the excitement that would have accompanied such a wonderful find. Imagine how the news would have spread around the world. How would we spread the news?

Generate: How many ideas can I think of?
How would the news have spread in November 1922? (Radio broadcasts began in November 1922.)

Decide: Which is the best idea?
Newspapers present the most efficient method of spreading the news.

Implement: Let's do it!
Split the class into five groups to work on a newspaper account of the discovery of Tutankhamun's tomb.
Group 1   Using Microsoft Publisher, write a leading article of the discovery of the tomb and the treasures within.
Group 2   Using Microsoft Publisher, write an account of the water boy's discovery of the stone steps.
Group 3   Using Microsoft Publisher, write an account of the quarrel with the Egyptian authorities over access to the tomb.
Group 4   Compile word and picture puzzles connected to the discovery.
Group 5   Produce cartoons and a comic strip account of the tomb's discovery.

Evaluate: How well did I do?
In groups consider individual contributions to the task.
Assemble the component parts of the newspapers.

Communicate: Let's tell someone!
Display the newspaper for others to read.
Post headline adverts around the building to draw attention to the newspaper.
Encourage children to write letters to the editor expressing their views on the finds.

Plenary

Learn from experience: What have I learned?
Produce a mindmap of everything that has been learned from this unit.

Notes/implications for future planning

English
En1   1b, 1e, 2b, 2e, 3a, 4c
En2   2a, 5a, 5f, 9a, 9b, 9c
En3   1a, 1e, 2a–f

ICT
1a, 2a, 3b, 4b, 5b

PSHE
1a, 2a, 2e, 2k, 4b

Vocabulary
archaeologist, artefact, museum, dig, find, tomb, seal, treasure

Differentiation
Tailor group allocation to children's strengths.

Support
Working with a supportive partner, extra input from the teacher.

Resources
Books on the tomb of Tutankhamun
Tape recorder
Computers

Key assessment
Is able to find out about the past from a range of sources of information.
Is able to ask and answer questions about the past.

Lesson plan Unit 3 (2 hours)

Date:	Curriculum area: History	Cross-curricular/ PSHE links
POS 1a, 1b, 2, 4, 5	**Learning objectives:** • to make deductions about the past from pictures of the landscape • to learn how much of the life of Egypt depended on the Nile	*English* En1 3a, 3b En3 1a, 1e, 2a–f

Introduction

Gather/organise: What do I already know about this?

Describe the location of UK and Egypt. Check descriptions against a globe.
Introduce/revise the term 'landscape' and write a definition.
Examine a collection of photographs and sort into 'UK', 'Egypt' or 'not sure'.
Watch BBC video *Egypt, Programme 1: The Gift of the Nile*. Check sorting of photographs.
Discuss the physical features of Egypt and the Nile. Consider: 'What was the Egyptian landscape like?' Examine photographs of UK. Discuss: 'What is our landscape like?'
Brainstorm ideas. Encourage and develop appropriate geographical vocabulary.

Activity

Identify: What is the task?
What does the landscape tell us about what life might have been like in ancient Egypt?

Generate: How many ideas can I think of?
How can we present this information? Discuss possible formats – annotated diagram, Venn diagram, grid, brainstorm, poster, leaflet, etc.

Decide: Which is the best idea?
Discuss options. Select individual/group formats.

Implement: Let's do it!
Record the elements of daily life that would have been made difficult/easy by the Egyptian landscape.

Evaluate: How well did I do?
Discuss whether the goal was achieved. What would I do differently next time?

Communicate: Let's tell someone!
Present information to the rest of the class. Discuss the variety of formats and the information conveyed.

Plenary

Learn from experience: What have I learned?

Discuss the new knowledge obtained during the lesson. Identify the recording formats used and consider when these might be used in other contexts.

Notes/implications for future planning

Geography
 1a, 2d, 3a, 3d, 3f

PSHE
 1a, 1b, 1c, 4b

Vocabulary
 landscape, river, desert, fertile, delta

Differentiation
 Encourage children to work creatively on a challenging format.

Support
 Working with a supportive partner, extra input from the teacher to model relevant procedures.

Resources
 Photographs of Egypt and of the locality
 Atlases
 BBC video *Egypt, Programme 1: The Gift of the Nile*

Key assessment
 Is able to make deductions about the past from pictures of the landscape.

Lesson plan Unit 4 (2 hours)

Date:	Curriculum area: History	Cross-curricular/ PSHE links

| POS 1a, 1b, 2, 4, 5 | **Learning objectives:**
• to classify information in various ways
• to learn about the range of objects which have survived from ancient Egypt
• to make inferences from objects about the way of life in ancient Egypt | *English*
En1 3a, 3b
En3 1a, 1e, 2a–f

Geography
1a, 2d, 3a, 3d, 3f |

Introduction

Explanation: We are going to learn about objects that survive from the time of the ancient Egyptians. We are going to classify them in a variety of ways and then consider what they tell us about the way of life in ancient Egypt.

Gather/organise: What do I already know about this?
Discuss: What objects do we know survive from the time of ancient Egypt? Why have these objects survived?

PSHE
1a, 1b, 1c, 4b

Vocabulary
landscape, river, desert, fertile, delta

Activity

Introduce pictures of ancient Egyptian objects.

Identify: What is the task?
How can we sort these objects?

Generate: How many ideas can I think of?
Ask the children to sort the pictures in different ways, e.g. Which are made from wood, paper, pottery, stone, etc.? Which tell us about food, death, daily life, clothes, houses? Which tell us about rich or poor people? Why?

What does the landscape tell us about what life might have been like in ancient Egypt?

How can we present this information? Discuss possible formats – annotated diagram, Venn diagram, grid, brainstorm, poster, leaflet, etc.

Decide: Which is the best idea?
Discuss options. Select individual/group formats.

Implement: Let's do it!
Record the elements of daily life that would have been made difficult/easy by the Egyptian landscape.

Evaluate: How well did I do?
Discuss whether the goal was achieved. What would I do differently next time?

Communicate: Let's tell someone!
Present information to the rest of the class. Discuss the variety of formats and the information conveyed.

Differentiation
Encourage children to work creatively on a challenging format.

Support
Working with a supportive partner, extra input from the teacher to model relevant procedures.

Resources
Photographs of Egypt and of the locality
Atlases
BBC video *Egypt, Programme 1: The Gift of the Nile*

Plenary

Learn from experience: What have I learned?
Discuss the new knowledge obtained during the lesson. Identify the recording formats used and consider when these might be used in other contexts.

Key assessment
Is able to make deductions about the past from pictures of the landscape.

Notes/implications for future planning

Lesson plan Unit 5 (2–3 hours)

Date:	Curriculum area: History	Cross-curricular/ PSHE links
POS 4a, 4b, 5a, 5b, 5c	**Learning objective:** • to observe an object in detail and to make inferences and deductions	*English* En1 3a–f En2 3a–e En3 1a, 1e, 2a–f

Introduction

Gather/organise: What do I already know about this?
Explore the ancient Egypt artefacts box (on loan from the local museum). Select and conceal an object from the rest of the table. Now describe it in detail so that it can be drawn without being seen. Compare results with artefacts and discuss the need for precise descriptions.

Activity
Discuss the work of archaeologists and historians. Explain that the most extensive collection of Egyptian artefacts outside Cairo is in the British Museum. We are going to visit the museum 'on-line' as assistants to help with the labelling of artefacts.
www.ancientegypt.co.uk/pharaoh/activity/main.html

Identify: What is the task?
Discuss the fact that what we know about the past is dependent on what has survived. Split the class into groups and give each group a topic, e.g. food and farming, art, buildings, writing, technology. Ask them to find three pictures and/or artefacts that they think can tell us the most about their topic.

Generate: How many ideas can I think of?
Ask the children to decide what they know for certain from their objects, what they can guess, and what they still need to find out.

Decide: Which is the best idea?
Discuss ways of presenting the information. Model the procedure with the children, using a favoured recording format.

Implement: Let's do it!
Ask the groups to record their observations and to extend their knowledge by using reference materials to find out more about their objects.

Evaluate: How well did I do?
Discuss how well groups worked together and how cooperation could have been improved.

Communicate: Let's tell someone!
The groups take turns to present their findings to the rest of the class.

Plenary

Learn from experience: What have I learned?
Reflect on the stages of the TASC Wheel and the TASC Thinking Tools used. Compare what we knew originally with what we know now. Examine the recording tool – when else could we use a similar idea?

Notes/implications for future planning

ICT 1a–c, 3a, 5a, 5b

PSHE 1a, 4b

Vocabulary
archaeologist, historian, artefact, museum, dig, find, tomb, seal, treasure, conservator, curator

Differentiation
Encourage children to work from a wide variety of sources.

Support
Working with a supportive partner, extra input from the teacher.

Resources
Ancient Egypt artefacts box Egypt project pack

Key assessment
Is able to present an artefact, making inferences and deductions about its use, in a discussion with others.

Lesson plan Unit 6 (2–3 hours)

Date:	Curriculum area: History	Cross-curricular/ PSHE links

POS 1a, 1b, 2, 4, 5	**Learning objectives:** • to learn about Egyptian tombs, pyramids and burial sites • to use sources of information in ways which go beyond simple observation

English
En1 3a–e
En2 2a, 2b, 3a–g
En3 1a–e, 2a–f

Introduction

Gather/organise: What do I already know about this?
Brainstorm what is already known about death, tombs, pyramids and burial sites and produce a mindmap, encouraging the grouping of ideas.
Discuss what questions could be asked to further extend this knowledge.
Shared reading: 'What did the ancient Egyptians believe about life after death?' (in *Ancient Egypt*, Jane Shuter, 2001, ISBN 0-431-10206-6).
Discuss the text and extend mindmap by adding new knowledge.

ICT
1a, 1b, 2a, 3a, 3b, 4a–c, 5b

PSHE
1a, 1c, 2a, 2e, 4b

Vocabulary
belief, death, tomb, pyramid, burial, site, archaeologist, artefact, exhibit, curator

Activity

Identify: What is the task?
Discuss the children's experience of museum visits. Explain the task – to create a museum display on ancient Egyptians' beliefs about the afterlife. Decide on the audience, perhaps children in the rest of the school. Discuss the key features of the exhibition.

Generate: How many ideas can I think of?
Collect pictures or objects which provide evidence about what the Egyptians believed about life after death or about what happened when people died. Discuss how to gather further information and how the information could be presented to the particular audience identified.

Decide: Which is the best idea?
Select the pictures or objects about death and mummification which could best be used to convey information to others. Plan how to proceed, by sharing tasks.

Implement: Let's do it!
Draw selected images and use research skills to produce captions giving interesting information for the audience to read.

Evaluate: How well did I do?
Discuss whether the necessary features of a museum exhibition have been achieved. Examine examples of good work. Discuss how efficiently the captions were produced – locating information, taking notes, drafting text, writing final captions.
Consider how to improve performance next time.

Communicate: Let's tell someone!
Mount a display of pictures, artefacts and captions on the after-life for other children to visit.

Differentiation
Increase the range of resource materials for more able children.

Support
Give children a fact sheet with captions to match with objects.

Resources
Books on ancient Egypt
Museum artefact pack
Reference materials
Computers

Plenary

Learn from experience: What have I learned?
Return to original mindmap, discuss and add newly acquired knowledge. Reflect on TASC Thinking Tools used.

Key assessment
Is able to present an artefact, making inferences and deductions about its use, in a discussion with others.

Notes/implications for future planning

Lesson plan Unit 7 (2–3 hours)

Date:	Curriculum area: HIstory	Cross-curricular/ PSHE links

| POS 2a, 4a, 5a, 5c | Learning objectives:
• to find out about ancient Egypt from what has survived
• to produce a structured account about life in ancient Egypt | *English*
En1 3a–e
En2 3a–g
En3 1a–e, 2a–f |

Introduction

Gather/organise: What do I already know about this?

Discuss with the children what they have learned about ancient Egypt. Organise the information into a mindmap. Discuss not only what is known but what is not known from what has survived.

Activity

Identify: What is the task?

Discuss the task with the children – to share their newly acquired knowledge with the rest of the school by producing a wall display on ancient Egypt covering all the topics they have learned about.

Generate: How many ideas can I think of?

Discuss the topics on ancient Egypt that they have studied. Re-examine the mindmaps. Do they need extending? Add any additional information.

Decide: Which is the best idea?

Discuss the best way of organising the setting up of a display. Discuss which areas to focus attention on and together allocate subject areas to groups, pairs or individuals. Consider the variety of formats the display could include.

Implement: Let's do it!

Split into groups, pairs, etc. to revise, research, draft and then present knowledge on ancient Egypt.

Evaluate: How well did I do?

Present completed work and decide if any pieces need re-doing before the display. Consider ways to improve individual pieces of work. Discuss how efficiently groups, pairs or individuals worked on their particular task and how this could be developed next time.

Communicate: Let's tell someone!

Draw together the information the children have produced to mount a display that shows understanding of the characteristic features of Egyptian society.

Plenary

Learn from experience: What have I learned?

Return to the mindmap produced in Unit 1 and compare with the most recent mindmap of acquired knowledge. Draw children's attention to the variety of recording techniques they have used. Reflect on TASK Thinking Tools used.

Notes/implications for future planning

ICT
1a, 1b, 2a, 3a, 3b, 4a–c, 5b

PSHE
1a, 1c, 2a, 4b

Vocabulary
All previous vocabulary

Differentiation
Increase the range of resource materials for more able children and encourage a variety of recording formats.

Support
Provide children with a frame to structure their writing.

Resources
Books on ancient Egypt
Museum artefacts pack
Reference materials
Computers

Key assessment
Is able to produce a structured account about life in ancient Egypt.

The children **gathered and organised** their existing knowledge by responding to the question, 'What do I already know about ancient Egypt?' Mindmaps, of varying complexity, were produced and discussed. Some misunderstandings were apparent, which the children were able to correct.

Next, we spent five minutes identifying questions the children would like to be able to answer to extend their knowledge.

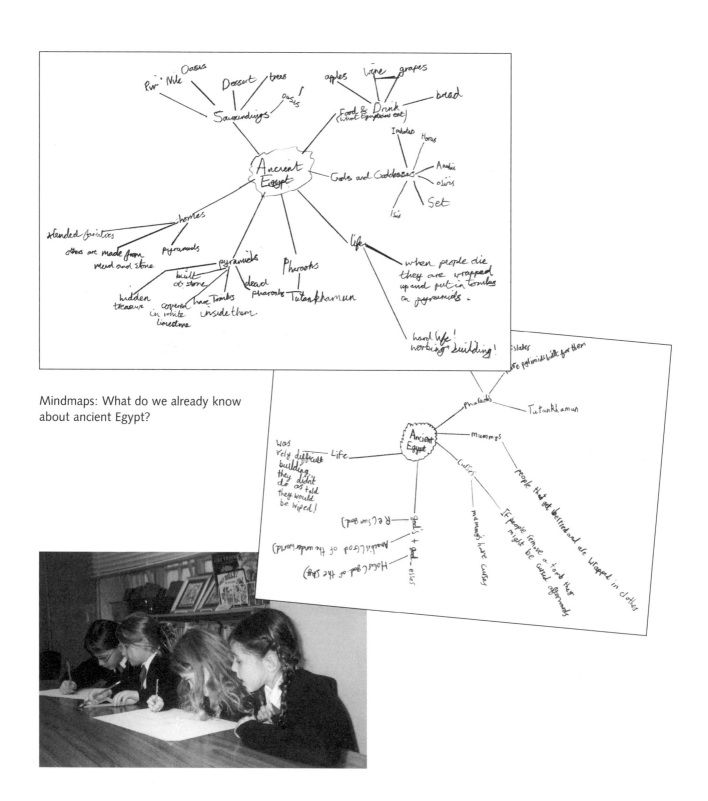

Mindmaps: What do we already know about ancient Egypt?

Did the ancient Egyptians go exploring?

What gods did they worship?

How long did it take to build a pyramid?

Where did the stone come from to build a pyramid?

How did the ancient Egyptians travel from place to place?

What clothes did the ancient Egyptians wear?

What equipment did they use for farming?

Did ancient Egyptian children go to school?

Did ancient Egyptian children have toys?

What was it like to be a pharaoh?

What did ancient Egyptians eat?

Did the ancient Egyptians have pets?

Did the ancient Egyptians play musical instruments?

Where did the ancient Egyptians buy things?

Did the ancient Egyptians only write in hieroglyphics?

What kind of weapons did the ancient Egyptians use in battle?

Did the ancient Egyptians have doctors and medicine?

What sort of houses did the ancient Egyptians have?

Did the ancient Egyptians have an army?

What else do we want to know about ancient Egypt?

We **identified** a sample question, 'What were schools like in ancient Egypt?' and applied it to the TASC Wheel. Initially we discussed the question – considering whether there were schools in ancient times. This proved to be a point of some debate – the children recalled the fact that boys went to school in Roman times as evidence that there could well have been schools in Egypt too. Others suggested that the ancient Egyptians lived long before the Romans and probably didn't have schools.

'How to find out' **generated** lots of ideas. We listed the possibilities – look in a book on ancient Egypt, find out on the Internet, phone the museum etc. The feasibility of each idea was discussed and then put in order of suitability. It was **decided** that a reference book was the most appropriate way to find out without leaving the classroom.

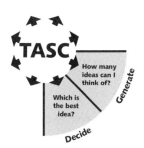

We **implemented** this decision by distributing books from the ancient Egypt project pack. Following a brief discussion on appraising non-fiction books for their usefulness, text was scanned and an answer to our question found.

Finding information

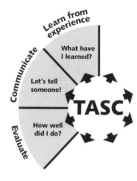

We **evaluated** our performance, discussing the appropriateness of selected key words and whether contents pages and headings were more or less useful than indexes.

We discussed possible ways of **communicating** this information to the rest of the year group before finally reflecting on what we had **learned from the experience**.

Unit 1

Learning objective

To locate ancient Egypt in time and place

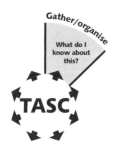

We discussed the learning objective and gathered together the children's existing knowledge. The general feeling was that Egypt was in Africa and that the pyramids, as the major symbol of ancient Egypt, were built thousands of years ago, certainly BC and possibly long before the Romans.

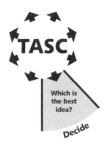

We decided to locate Egypt as a place first – we felt more confident of its physical location. None of the children had visited Egypt, although several had relatives and neighbours who had. We asked ourselves the question, 'What is Egypt like?' The responses were relatively limited – the consensus of opinion was that it was a hot, dusty place in Africa with pyramids and camels. We examined a varied collection of postcards and photographs. This confirmed the children's initial ideas but also introduced the notion of bustling modern city life and fertile farmland.

Locating Egypt on the globe

Africa was located on a globe and then Egypt was quickly sited. We discussed the use of atlases to find maps and worked our way from the contents page first to a world map and then to a more detailed map of north Africa. We pored over the place names and the physical features. An interesting misunderstanding arose – some children, despite a study of rivers in the previous term, believed that the Nile flowed 'down the page', from north to south. This gave other children the opportunity to act as experts, explaining that rivers always flow downhill to the sea. This discussion was followed by the positioning of Upper and Lower Egypt

Working on a map of ancient Egypt

on the children's photocopied maps. We looked at a variety of prepared maps, showing the pyramids, the Valley of the Kings, Abu Simbel, the deserts, Nubia etc., briefly discussing the country's natural defences and the location of settlements along the course of the river.

Next, we turned our attention to locating ancient Egypt in time. We consolidated understanding of AD and BC dates, taking a long length of string and hanging an '0' decorated with nativity scenes near the middle. We discussed Biblical events around this time – the Flight into Egypt and the earlier stories of Moses. We then practised counting forwards and backwards across '0'. We discussed major events in our recent history and wondered how long ago the ancient Egyptians had lived.

We brainstormed major ancient Egyptian events like the building of the pyramids and the death of Tutankhamun. Pictures connected with these events were put onto a whiteboard and the children were invited to use the resources of the library to find relevant dates. Good library skills were evident as the children located appropriate texts, scanned contents pages and indexes, accessed encyclopaedias and CD-ROM reference sites.

Accessing the information

The illustrations, with their approximate dates, were put into chronological order and the span of the timeline calculated. It was decided to place thousand year markers on to our timeline, from AD2000 to 3000BC at one metre intervals. The children calculated that each centimetre would represent ten years. The illustrations of the pyramids, Abu Simbel etc., were hung from the timeline using treasury tags at the appropriate points.

The children were shown illustrations of major historical events and asked to name others. Again we put the pictures on the whiteboard and again the children scoured reference materials to assign dates to each image. In pairs, the children took an event, located it on the timeline by careful measuring and hung it in place.

Working on the timeline

The timeline became over-crowded in the last millennium. We considered why this should be the case. They felt that this was because of the growth of technology and cited examples of change over recent years and by referring to conversations with parents and especially grandparents. They also felt that we know more about the recent past because of the increased availability of books and newspapers, the advent of film and television and because of the memories of very old people who lived long ago.

It was decided that the timeline needed thinning out a little. We took out everything between 1800 and 2002 and lay the illustrated dates in order. We asked ourselves the question, 'Which are the most important events?' This was an interesting exercise – the children generally omitted events that had little direct bearing on their own lives, e.g. the World Wars, while including those events that touched them directly, e.g. the appearance of TV sets across the country. They had prioritised their thoughts after reflecting on the relative importance they attached to each event. We wondered if our parents and grandparents would have chosen the same events and resolved to discuss the question at home.

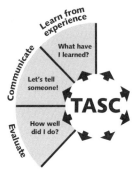

We examined the completed timeline, reflected on how long ago the ancient Egyptians lived, discussed which were the best resources for finding dates quickly and evaluated how well we had worked with our partners. We rounded off the afternoon by summarising what we had learned. It was generally felt that the knowledge gained about the physical location of Egypt was predictable like the 'next page in a textbook', but the location in time, although they had previously worked on personal timelines, was a completely new topic. The lesson had enabled the children to select and prioritise and to sequence the events. We completed the lesson by discussing these 'thinking tools'.

Now it was time to share the timeline with another class. This had to wait until the following day. The children enthusiastically showed off their work, confidently explaining the steps they had taken.

Completed timeline

The activities had extended the children's experiences across the interpersonal and logical/mathematical intelligences.

Unit 2

Learning objectives

To ask and answer questions about the past

To find out about the past from a range of sources of information

 Because of the quantity of work involved in Unit 2, it was decided to cover the background to the discovery of Tutankhamun's tomb in English lessons. First of all, we located the Pharaoh's burial and discovery on the timeline and discussed how we find out about the past.

The Tomb of Tutankhamun (Mason 1991) was introduced as a class text, read in instalments and discussed over the course of a few days. We also studied photocopied diary entries relating to the discovery and used search engines on the Internet to obtain extra information.

 The key events were identified and arranged in sequence then a flow chart was produced outlining the story. We practised our note-making techniques, marking extracts by annotating and by selecting key headings, words or sentences. We made short notes by abbreviating ideas, selecting key words, listing ideas and by drawing labelled diagrams.

Using a tape recorder we recorded the 'hot seating' of a variety of characters – Howard Carter, Lord Carnarvon, Egyptian workers, the water boy, journalists and other archaeologists. The children have lots of experience of 'hot seating' and tackled the interaction with gusto. In order to answer the many varied questions, those in the hot seat had to recall quite detailed information – a task they achieved with confidence.

These activities gave experience across the linguistic and interpersonal intelligences.

How did you feel when you discovered the tomb?
I was hot and tired but as soon as I saw the first step I thought this must be somebody's tomb. When I actually opened the door I saw wonderful things and it was just amazing. There was millions of treasure and we went to the second room and we saw special markings. It was just amazing.

What was your favourite item in the room?
It was this very good vase. It was very good quality, it didn't have any gold in it but it had loads of markings on it. That was the best favoured. Everyone was asking for that one. Maybe I'll just put it in a museum so that everyone can admire it.

How many days have you been working on the job?
I've been working on the job since 1917, that's five years.

Were you starting to feel hopeless when you couldn't find anything?
Everybody was giving up, yes. We were starting to lose our hope but we kept on working. We were determined to find something or else we thought it would be a waste of money.

Did you actually find the tomb?
I think I did. I'm not sure if it was one of my workers. The water boy discovered the first step. The water boy should get most of the credit because it was him who led us to the tomb.

What did you feel like when you didn't find anything?
We were starting to be very tired of digging and having no profit. We were really hot and sweaty and bothered and there were lots of arguments in the tents.

While you were digging did you find anything else?
We just found some useless pottery. It was not valuable at all.

Where you amazed when you saw the golden death mask?
Yes I was amazed. I was very shocked. All my workers who were working for me were really shocked about all the gold because they've never seen as much gold as that in their lives.

What did the young king look like?
He's dead so we couldn't really tell what he looked like! It was just a skeleton. I'm sure he looked a bit better when he was actually alive. The death mask gave us an idea of what he looked like. It was a head-dress and it was gold with blue glass on it.

Where did you find the tomb?
I found it in 1922 on November the third in the Valley of the Kings.

Interviewing Howard Carter

Learning objectives

To ask and answer questions about the past

To find out about the past from a range of sources of information

 We reviewed our flow chart and discussed the excitement that would have accompanied such a wonderful find. We imagined how the news would have spread around the world – by word of mouth, by letter, by newspaper, by radio, by telephone by telegraph, perhaps even by pigeon. We considered how we would spread the news today and compared the two brainstorms. Then we turned our attention back to 1922/1923 and considered how the largest audience could be reached. We discussed Howard Carter's decision to give reporting rights to just one newspaper, *The Times*, and how it had caused uproar among the world's press.

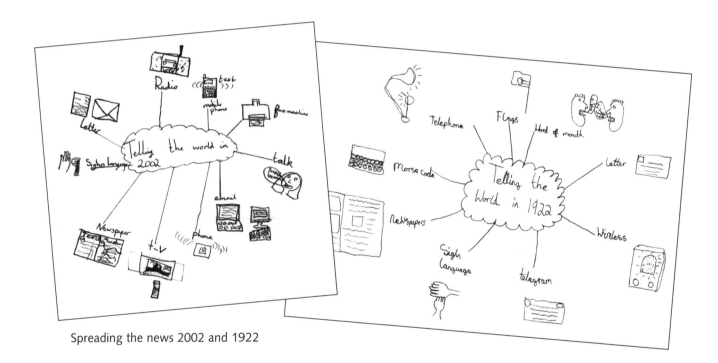

Spreading the news 2002 and 1922

We set about the task of informing the rest of the school by newspaper of Howard Carter's discoveries. We split into groups of six. Group 1 used Microsoft 'Publisher' to fill out their brief notes into connected prose by writing leading articles of the discovery of the tomb and the treasures within. Group 2 used 'Publisher' and wrote accounts of the water boy's discovery of the stone steps. Group 3 used 'Publisher' to write an account of the quarrel with the Egyptian authorities over access to the tomb. Group 4 compiled word and picture puzzles connected to the discovery. Group 5 produced cartoons and a comic strip account of the tomb's discovery.

Using 'Publisher' to write a newspaper article

The groups using 'Publisher' found working to a specific space quite challenging. Making their articles 'fit the space' produced much discussion and on-screen editing. Adding illustrations took a great deal of time. The children generally couldn't find clip art pictures that appealed to them so opted for a search of Internet sites. They were disappointed not to find photographs of Howard Carter and the 1922/1923 discoveries, despite a lengthy search. With time running out, it was decided to use the resource books and the photocopier and literally 'cut and paste'.

The word puzzle group decided to work in pairs to construct crossword puzzles, a wordsearch and a coded message. The crossword and wordsearch pairs began by listing words connected with the great discovery and writing them as interlocking words. Having finally produced a grid they were happy with, the crossword pairs set about writing the clues. This gave rise to much debate over the difficulty level involved. A compromise was reached when it was decided to produce two crosswords – one easy and one more difficult puzzle.

Testing the crossword puzzle

Wordsearch puzzle

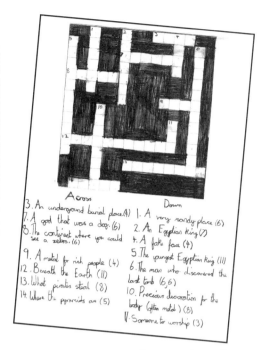

Crossword puzzle

The cartoonists started by agreeing on a six-picture strip. After much deliberation they agreed on key events for each block and entered the text before setting to work on the illustrations.

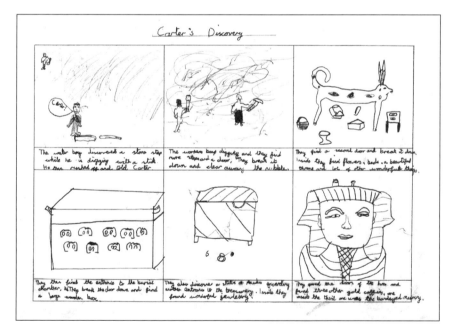

Cartoon strip

The compilation of the newspaper was done a few days after the history lesson when the separate parts were all finished. Banner headlines were discussed, produced and displayed and resulted in much interest from the rest of the year group.

The plenary focused on what had been learned and how it had been learned. *The various activities had extended experience across the linguistic, visual/spatial, interpersonal and intrapersonal intelligences.*

Learning objective

(English Year 4 Term 2)

To develop use of settings in own writing, making use of work on adjectives and figurative language to describe settings effectively

In our extended writing lesson, we were investigating story settings and decided to extend this work to our history study.

 We examined photographs of the setting of Howard Carter's 'dig' of November 1922 and brainstormed adjectives and figurative language connected with the scenes. The children confidently imagined themselves in the desert location, calling upon recently acquired knowledge about the dig and personal experiences of being in very hot locations on family holidays.

We discussed the excited, enthusiastic diary entries that Howard Carter had made after the discovery of Tutankhamun's tomb and wondered what the entries made before the 'find' would have been like. We contrasted his later exhilarated state with that of a despondent man whose dream of finding Tutankhamun's tomb was in danger of being abandoned. We imagined how Howard Carter would have felt as he sat down to write his diary after yet another fruitless day in the field, with the possibility of funding being withdrawn. The children were totally absorbed in this task, displaying some understanding of the emotional and physical strain that must have been evident at the time.

'Aging' the paper with a damp teabag fascinated the children and they were eager to show their authentic looking documents to children in other classes.

We shared the diary entries and discussed the thoughts that made some particularly successful. The children had successfully put themselves in someone else's shoes in considering Carter's point of view and *had further contact with the linguistic and intrapersonal intelligences.*

Extracts from Howard Carter's diary

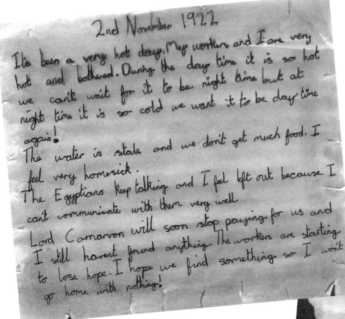

Diary extracts

2nd November 1922

It's been a very hot day. My workers and I are very hot and bothered. During the day time it is so hot we can't wait for it to be night time but at night time it is so cold we want it to be day time again!
The water is stale and we don't get much food. I feel very homesick.
The Egyptians keep talking and I feel left out because I can't communicate with them very well.
Lord Carnarvon will soon stop paying for us and I still haven't found anything. The workers are starting to lose hope. I hope we find something so I won't go home with nothing!

2nd November 1922

We've just wasted another day. Nothing has been found. The temperature has gone saving up.

I've just recived a letter from Lord Carnarvon. It says if we don't find something soon he will stop paying the bills. Me and the workers are starting to loose hope. I'll be suprised if we find anything.

Although I don't know what the workers are saying I think they're about to give up. I really hope we find something, and soon.

Learning objective

(English Year 4 Term 2)

To collect information from a variety of sources and present it in one simple format, e.g. wall chart, labelled diagram

This was one of our learning objectives in the week following the work on the discovery of Tutankhamun's tomb. In our introductory shared writing session, we examined a variety of wall charts, posters and diagrams in books and discussed other formats we had experienced in the past. We shared the learning objective and discussed how we could present the collected information on Howard Carter and Tutankhamun. Initially, the children referred to the formats we had just scrutinised, noting where the format was suitable and where it was flawed, before moving on to suggest variations of their own. Relating the events in a flow chart was a popular option, so together we modelled how this might be done. We recapped on the variety of other possible layouts and the children sketched out their ideas on rough paper. Independent group work over the course of the week was devoted to the completion of this task. The children were focused throughout. They returned to a variety of sources for information, made notes, drafted and improved their text, before finally presenting their work.

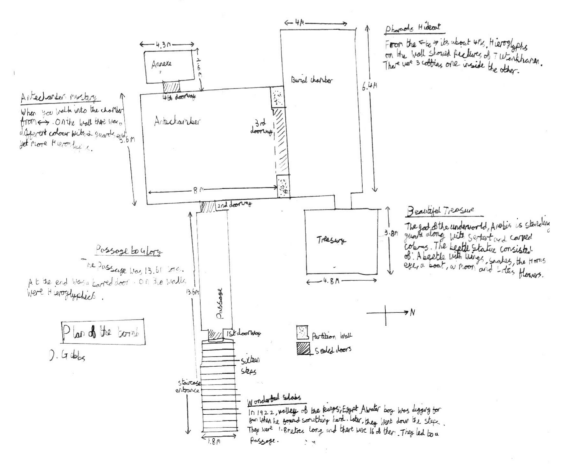

Plan of Tutankhamun's tomb (D's work)

One can see the difference in style in the two plans of Tutankhamun's tomb. M's work is spatially accurate, while D's work is linguistically detailed.

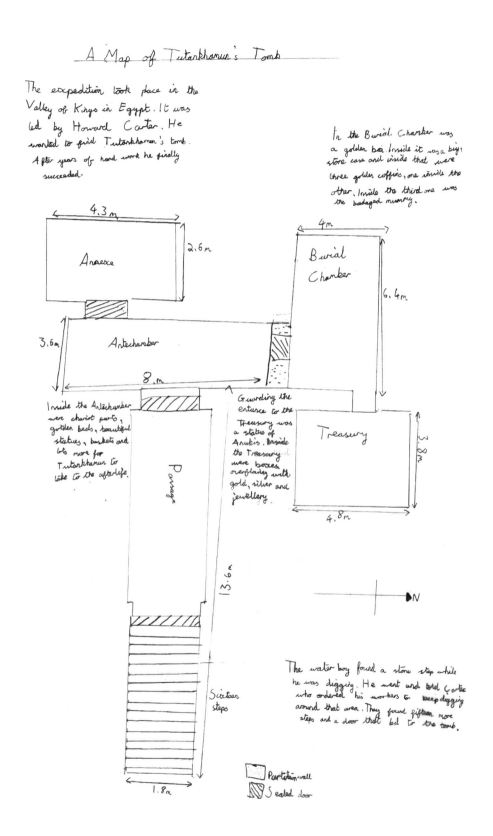

Plan of Tutankhamun's tomb (M's work)

Unit 3

Learning Objectives

To make deductions about the past from pictures of the landscape

To learn how much of the life of Egypt depended on the Nile

 The children were encouraged to describe the location of UK and Egypt without the aid of globes and atlases. After a slow start, they were able to confirm their positions in the northern hemisphere and their compass positions relative to other countries, seas etc. These descriptions were then checked against a globe.

The term 'landscape' was recorded on the blackboard and a definition elicited from the children. A collection of landscape photographs were viewed and sorted into 'UK', 'Egypt' or 'not sure' as appropriate. It was explained to the class that we were about to watch a video about Egypt and the River Nile in which they should pay particular attention to information about the landscape and land usage.

After the programme, we used a mindmap to organise the information we had received. The terms 'arid' and 'temperate' were introduced.

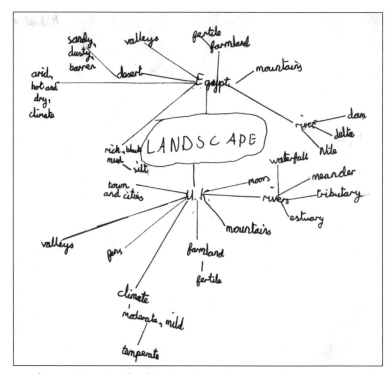

Mindmap: Comparing landscapes

We discussed how the type of landscape affected the daily life of its inhabitants. This discussion developed into thinking about what we like and dislike in our lives and what we would have liked or disliked about living in ancient Egypt. We considered ways in which this information could be presented. A number of possible formats were suggested – brainstorms, grids, Venn diagrams, posters, leaflets, newspaper articles and advertisements. After further discussion in groups, the children settled to the recording task.

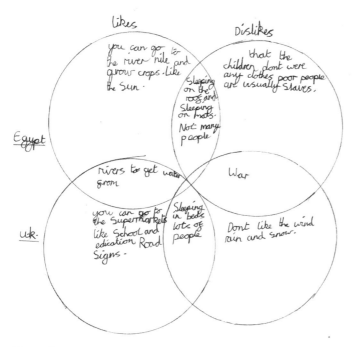

Venn diagram

Poster

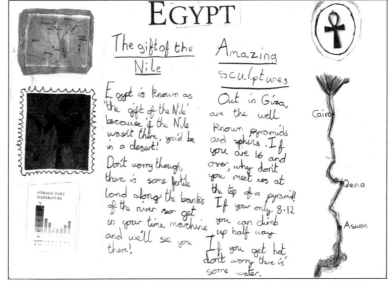

Leaflet

In evaluating the task, the children felt that they had achieved their goal of deciding which elements of daily life would have been made easy or difficult by living at the time of the ancient Egyptians. They felt that both sides of the situation were investigated, by having put themselves into someone else's shoes. However, they felt that only some of their reasons were directly related to the landscape and if done again, they felt it was important to keep strictly to the landscape issue.

Information was shared with the class. The likes and dislikes represented caused some considerable debate. In conclusion we considered the question, 'What if the Nile suddenly changed its course away from Egypt?' The consensus was that the people would have to follow it, wherever it went because their lives depended completely on the river.

The variety of formats presented was quite impressive and provided the focal point of the plenary. We discussed what had worked well and when we might have used similar ideas on previous pieces of work.

The linguistic, logical / mathematical, visual / spatial and interpersonal intelligences were visited during this lesson.

Unit 4

Learning objectives

To classify information in various ways

To learn about the range of objects which have survived from ancient Egypt

To make inferences from objects about the way of life in ancient Egypt

We began, as usual, by discussing the learning objectives and the intended outcomes. The introduction was relatively brief. The children already had a good working knowledge of the sort of objects that survive from ancient times. In the opening discussion they listed the materials they expected objects to be made from and most were quite clear that they wouldn't find any modern materials such as plastic.

Examining artefacts

A collection of photographs and a museum pack of Egyptian artefacts were inspected by the children.

They suggested one or two set labels for classification and swiftly set about sorting, adding more sets as the need arose. Initially, there was a tendency to work almost individually. Sets for 'metal', 'gold' and 'silver' appeared and it took a little while for the children to subsume the sets into one. Much discussion, relocating and overlapping of sets was evident. The children finally stood back to evaluate their performance. They were pleased with the classifications they had made. Their expectations were confirmed – many objects were made of stone, metal, bone and clay, but they were surprised by the survival of objects made from reeds. In reflecting on performance, they acknowledged that the activity would have been completed more quickly if they had cooperated better as a team from the start.

Sorting pictures and artefacts into sets

On-line at the British Museum

In our next lesson, we discussed the fact that what we know about the past is dependent on what has survived. We recapped briefly the sort of objects and materials which had survived from the time of ancient Egypt. Then we split into groups and each group chose a topic of interest to them, eg. food and farming, art, buildings, weapons, technology. They were asked to find three pictures and/or artefacts that they thought could tell us the most about their topic. The children were highly selective in their choices. We had the museum artefacts pack and the collection of photographs from the sorting exercise, but most groups copied one or two of their objects from the reference materials in the classroom.

Finding pictures and artefacts
that told about a particular topic

It was explained that we were about to build a different sort of mindmap to those we usually compiled. We wanted to sort our knowledge into three categories – 'what we know for certain from the objects', 'what we can guess', and 'what we still need to find out'.

We discussed ways of presenting information in this way – the children were eager to explain their ideas and drew rough sketches of layouts on the board. To model the procedure, we chose pictures of three musical instruments. The categories 'what we know for certain' and 'what we can guess' proved to be a source of debate. Eventually, it was decided that in order to be 'known for certain' a fact had to be unanimously agreed upon, otherwise it fell into the 'we can guess' category. The children were very 'free flowing' and imaginative with their thoughts about 'what we still need to find out'.

Feeling confident, the groups settled busily to the task. They chose a recording format for their observations and extended their knowledge by using reference materials to answer their questions. It was pleasing to overhear one child encouraging another to put himself into the shoes of an ancient Egyptian and of another who suggested looking at a particular question from the opposite point of view.

Death

What we know for certain . . . death

What we know for certain . . . weapons

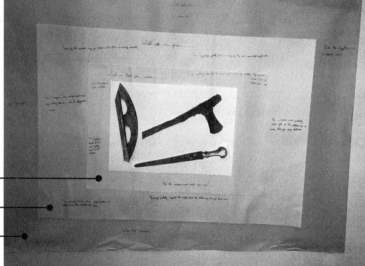

what we know for certain ————

what can we guess ————

what we still need to find out ————

Weapons

What we need to find out

Were they
expensive?

Did the Egyptians
invade or defend land?

What we can guess

They probably trained
soldiers before battle
but maybe sent them
straight into battle.

The weapons were
probably quite light as
the soldiers carried them
long distances.

Some of the
weapons may
have killed people
while others
seriously
wounded.

How did
the
weapons
kill?

What we know for certain

All weapons
were made for
war.

The Egyptians must
have had wars.

All the
weapons
were hand
held.

WEAPONS

How
were the
weapons
made?

The weapons
were
perhaps kept
sharp by
rubbing them
on stone.

The handles
were made of
metal and
wood.

The cutting edges of
the axes were made
of metal.

The Egyptians
probably had
a huge army.

Weapons

In the evaluation into how well the group members had worked together, it was noted that the most effective groups worked together as a group, bouncing ideas off each other, until the final questions needed answering when they worked individually or in pairs. The less effective groups, it was discovered, split into ones and twos much earlier and physically achieved less. The groups enjoyed presenting their findings about life in ancient Egypt to the rest of the class and took the opportunity to add further questions from the class to their recording sheets.

We reflected on the stages of the TASC Wheel that had been visited and of the TASC Thinking Tools we had used. Each group reported back on one new piece of information that they had acquired. We examined the recording formats we had selected, considering what had worked well and when else we could use similar ideas.

These analytical and creative thinking activities had extended the children once more in to the logical and visual/spatial intelligences.

Unit 6

Learning objectives

To learn about Egyptian tombs, pyramids and burial sites

To use sources of information in ways which go beyond simple observation

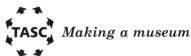 *Making a museum*

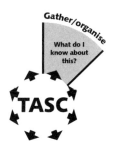

Illustrations of a pyramid, a mummy and a funeral procession were placed in the centre of a whiteboard. The children chose 'Death' as a mindmap title and began to brainstorm what was already known about the subject. Most of the class automatically proposed sub-headings as the next step while the remainder still needed encouraging to group their ideas. The headings 'Pyramids', 'Tombs', 'Mummies', 'Gods' and 'The After-life' were chosen initially and further ideas and details cascaded from these starting points. As the discussion proceeded, 'Pyramids', 'Tombs' and a further section on 'Temples' became sub-headings of 'Burial places'.

We considered what questions could be asked to further extend this knowledge. The children were eager to know more about the preparation of bodies, the journey into the after-life and the roles of different gods in the process.

Together we read the section, 'What did the ancient Egyptians believe about life after death?' from *Ancient Egypt* by Jane Shuter (2001, ISBN 0-431-10206-6). We discussed the text and extended the mindmap by adding new knowledge in a different colour. A suggestion was made that the title needed changing because it gave the impression of a final 'ending'. 'Death – the continuing story' was highly rated by the more able members of the class, although 'Death and the after-life' was the most popular replacement idea, with 'Journey into the after-life' being proposed as the new sub-heading to stand in lieu of 'The after-life'.

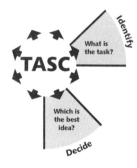

We selected death-related items from the museum loan pack. The children were encouraged to recall their experiences of museum visits. They related their fascination with exhibits, their frustration at not being able to handle items encased in glass and the difficulty of reading explanatory texts accompanying the items. The discussion was extended to consider a 'perfect children's museum'. They were quick to suggest the key features – everything could be handled, it didn't have to be quiet, the supporting information had to be simple and easy to read, there needed to be lots of colourful illustrations and maps and there had to be a fun quiz, preferably with a prize.

We contemplated the task – to create a museum display on ancient Egyptians' beliefs about the after-life. We decided on the audience – children in the rest of the school – and a place for the exhibition – the school library. The organisation of an exhibition was enthusiastically discussed: the children proposed favourite artefacts, illustrations and reference materials to use and even suggested a rota of museum attendants. We reviewed how to gather further information and how the information could be presented to the audience.

Reference materials were distributed for the task of selecting the pictures about death and mummification which could best be used to convey information to others. We listed and prioritised the items – mummies, canopic jars, shabtis, amulets etc. and then drew up a plan of how to proceed, by sharing tasks.

The children used their research skills to note key words and phrases, to fill out brief notes into connected prose and after re-drafting, to produce interesting captions for the audience to read. Where we had no artefact, the children drew selected images. Another group set themselves the task of producing a quiz sheet, based on the research work being done by others, while one small group listened to Egyptian music and made their own taped version of background music for the exhibition.

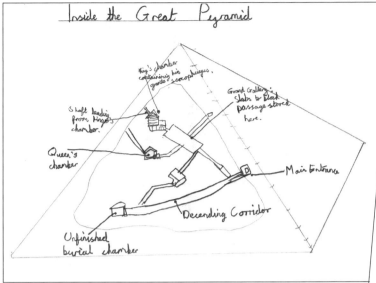

Inside the Great Pyramid

King's chamber containing his granite sarcophagus.

Shaft leading from King's chamber

Queen's chamber

Grand Gallery: Slabs to block passage stored here.

Main Entrance

Descending Corridor

Unfinished burial chamber

Pyramids

Music making

We came together to discuss whether the basis of a museum exhibition had been achieved. We examined examples of good illustrative and written work and discussed the suitability of captions – ensuring they were informative and easy to read. Concern was expressed over some children's handwriting so it was decided to print all captions on the computer. With this amendment in hand, it was decided that the exhibition could take place.

Pyramids

Pyramids took many years to build and thousands of workers helped. Roughly 2.3m blocks were used. Only early pharaohs had pyramids. The later pharaohs had underground tombs to keep out grave robbers. Another reason is that they were cheaper and easier to build.

The main entrance of the Great Pyramid at Giza was 18 m high. Each side was 230 m long! Inside was only four rooms. Pharaoh Khufu was buried inside the Great Pyramid, but the weird thing is there were three burial chambers in the pyramid! One was for his granite sarcophagus (a stone box that the coffin lay in) and one unfinished.

But why pyramids? One reason is that the structure lasts. It's very solid and has lasted for thousands of years. Why did they build them so big? The Egyptians probably wanted to show their power to other people. The pyramids of Giza are one of the Seven Wonders of the World. They have towered above the people of Egypt for thousands of years and will probably continue to do so for thousands of years more.

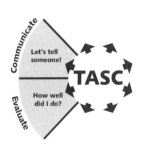

We pondered how to improve performance next time. Buying a school mummy was not really an option! However, the children also thought that extending the school's own artefact pack would be a good idea. A few children admitted to being tempted to copy straight from reference materials rather than having the confidence to make the text their own – a problem which was understood and appreciated by many, although much helpful and encouraging advice was offered by the children themselves.

We returned to the original mindmap. The research done for the captions had extended our knowledge further. Children reported back their findings, these were discussed and added to the mindmap in a third colour.

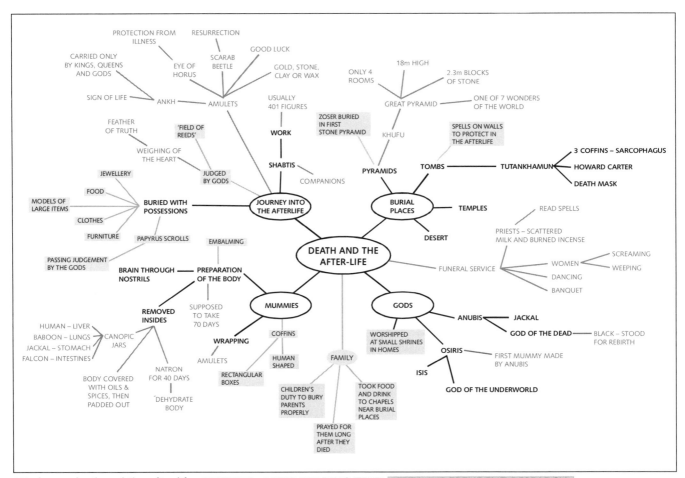

Mindmap: death and the after-life: ORIGINAL, AFTER READING TEXT, AFTER INDEPENDENT RESEARCH

Reflecting on the TASC Thinking Tools used was the final step – we had looked at the issues from **both sides**, we had thought **in all directions**, considering the needs of others, we had put things **in order of importance** and we had used our mindmapping to **make links**. In addition, the children planned to **ask other people** for feedback about their exhibition.

Exhibition

A display of pictures, artefacts and captions on the after-life was mounted a week later, for other children to visit. The children took turns in acting as museum attendants, ensuring careful handling of the artefacts and answering questions.

This exhibition and the work leading up to it had given the opportunity to use the linguistic, logical, visual/spatial, musical, interpersonal and intrapersonal intelligences.

Learning objectives

(English Year 4 Term 2)

To understand the use of figurative language in poetry; locate use of simile

To write poetry based on the structure and/or style of poems read, e.g. taking account of vocabulary, archaic expressions, patterns of rhyme, choruses, similes

While Unit 6 was being undertaken, it was 'Book Week' in our school. The focus for the week was poetry – an enjoyable change in a half term dominated by non-fiction texts. A number of visiting speakers stimulated the children's imagination with readings of poetry and prose. In class, the children eagerly read and discussed their favourite poems.

It was a wet February morning when we read 'Spell of the Rain' by Leslie Norris (Masson *et al.* 1983). We studied the structure and the language of the poem and then imagined what it would be like in Egypt. Using the structure of the poem as a framework, the children were asked to write poetry on the sun.

On the subsequent day we looked at a variety of poems containing similes. We listed words to describe what the river Nile does – flows, floods, glistens etc. using a thesaurus when we ran out of ideas. After that we found images for the river using similes. We collaborated in writing a short poem, then the children worked in pairs to draft their own versions.

The children were eager to write a poem about Tutankhamun. We read an assortment of evocative poems, focused attention on his gleaming death mask and brainstormed descriptive words and phrases. We discussed the type of poem we might write and whether to work individually or in pairs. The final decision was left with the children themselves. Most children used the brainstorming ideas to write descriptively, some chose to attempt rhyming poems, and a few, not grasping the ideas securely, wrote prose in short lines.

We completed the week by taking our three poems and presenting them in pyramid shaped books. *Creating anthologies had been a further venture into the linguistic and visual/spatial multiple intelligences.*

Pyramid books

Images of the Nile

The Nile
  Reflects
like a looking glass
  Flows
like a blue ballgown
  Rushes
like a gleaming diamond falling down a
shimmering waterfall
  Glistens
like tiny stars in the inky sky
  Slides
like a precious snake
  Ripples
like an emerald fish
  Drips
like small pearl drops

Spell of the Sun

Blazing
  rays of ferocious light
The blistering sun
  shining down on massive pyramids
The scorching sun
  roasting the backs of tired workers
The dazzling sun
  sparkling down on the sphinx
The powerful sun
  burning the people of Egypt
The ferocious light
  is dazzling

Death Mask

Tutankhamun's mask is very old
Made of blue glass and solid gold
It was buried years ago
And belonged to a very young pharaoh
The rest of his story will soon be told
And his mysterious death will then unfold

Unit 7

Learning objectives

To find out about ancient Egypt from what has survived

To produce a structured account about life in ancient Egypt

After an explanation that the ancient Egypt project was drawing to a close, we discussed what the children had learned. We talked about not only what was known but also what was not known from what had survived. For example, the children felt they now knew plenty about the daily life of ancient Egyptians, but wondered what their language and music actually sounded like.

We considered how we could organise such a quantity and variety of information in a limited amount of time. The children unanimously called for a mindmap and immediately began suggesting sub-headings – 'People', 'Buildings', 'Nile', 'Art' etc. Paper was distributed and a time limit was set. The children paired up to construct their mindmaps, enthusiastically and efficiently 'bouncing ideas' off each other. Facts in dispute were quickly checked against information in history folders, on the classroom display or in reference materials.

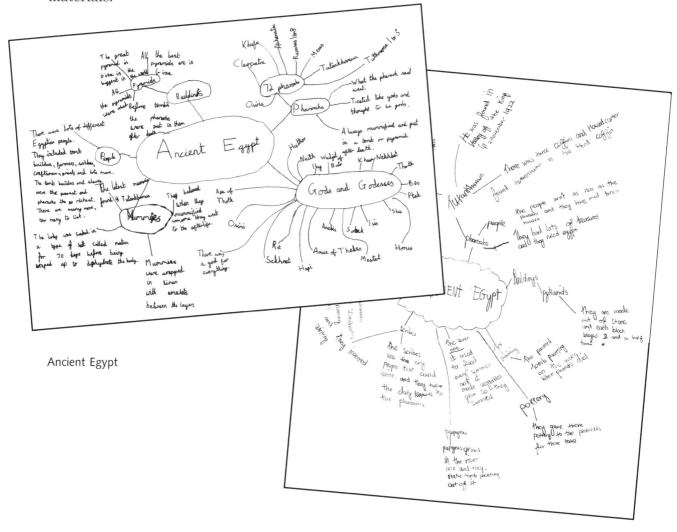

Ancient Egypt

After 15 minutes, we discussed which had been the most fruitful sub-headings and which areas had been more challenging. They concluded that most areas were quite plentiful in information which had been easy to recall, but they were disappointed that they had not had the opportunity to spend more time finding out about 'Gods and Goddesses'. Many children had undertaken their own research on the subject and we had read and illustrated a few myths connected to our work in art, but clearly this had not been enough. I promised to take this shortcoming into account when planning for the project next time.

Illustrations of the myth 'Isis and Osiris'

We used the children's mindmaps to produce a compilation of class knowledge. This triggered fresh recollections and the mindmap became extensive with numerous links between sub-headings.

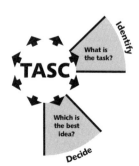

Feeling rather pleased at the extent of their knowledge, the children discussed the task before them – to produce a display on ancient Egypt covering all the areas they had studied. They were excited at the prospect of organising their own display. A deluge of ideas was put forward. It took a few minutes, but eventually one practical soul recognised that we needed a plan.

The children divided themselves into groups of varying sizes, each group assigned to a particular sub-heading on the class mindmap. They elected chairpersons, collected appropriate work from their folders and discussed what else was needed for the final display. Working individually or in pairs, some children identified areas of limited knowledge, e.g. 'Gods' and made notes, then drafted, improved and presented their text, while others decided to improve previous pieces of work.

We reflected on the afternoon session. The communication segment of the TASC Wheel remained to be completed, but that was in hand. We had worked successfully, using the TASC Framework and TASC Thinking Tools for support and had achieved our intended outcomes. We took out our first ancient Egypt mindmaps and marvelled at how much more everyone now knew about ancient Egypt.

Lunchtimes were used to complete the presentation. Photographs, of the children's work at varying stages, were offered for inclusion in their display. The children chose sandy colours for mounting and, with supervision, they managed to trim their own work and single mount it. After a little trimming and double mounting the work was ready for the display boards. The children enjoyed experimenting with different layouts and soon arrived at a display with which they were happy.

The display took pride of place on the school stage and was eagerly examined by the school family of pupils, parents and staff. Numerous praiseworthy comments were received which were relayed to the children. The response to the admiration was mixed. Some were of the attitude 'quite right too', but the majority were critical of the display, offering suggestions about what they would do differently next time.

This final display had given the opportunity to use the linguistic, logical, visual/spatial, interpersonal and intrapersonal intelligences.

Final display

Conclusion

REFLECT

Our initial aim of developing problem-solving and thinking skills using the TASC paradigm and the QCA Ancient Egypt unit of study (QCA/DfEE 2000) had been achieved.

The children had found out about the way of life of people living in ancient Egypt from archaeological discoveries. They had developed their understanding of characteristic features of a society; identified the different ways the past is represented; and used sources of information to make simple observations, inferences and deductions.

As a class teacher, I found TASC extremely supportive in both the planning stage and in the actual delivery to the children – leading us all confidently to the next step. Just as the children consider what they would do differently next time, I also reflect critically. I plan to re-assess our medium-term planning to further develop cross-curricular links, especially in music, drama and design technology (DT). This would give more scope to the inclusion of the musical and bodily kinaesthetic intelligences which, although included in other aspects of the curriculum, were not as prominent as they could be in our history study.

TASC had provided the supportive framework for 'average' and 'below average' children to perform with increasing confidence, while enabling 'above average' children to work quite independently. The children's organisation and articulation of existing knowledge was much improved, they were much more focused about the precise task in hand, ideas flowed from them with greater spontaneity and there was an improvement in their ability to listen to each other's proposals. They thrived on being involved in the planning and decision-making process and they extended their repertoire of recording techniques across the multiple intelligences. They became more comfortable with self-assessment issues, more confident when sharing their work with an audience and much more aware of exactly what they had learned and how they might transfer the learning to other situations.

References and resources

For children

Allan, T. (1997) *Pharaohs and Pyramids*. London: Usborne.
British Museum Website www.ancientegypt.co.uk/pharaoh/activity/main.html
Defrates, J. (1991) *What Do We Know About the Egyptians?* London: Simon & Schuster.
Ganeri, A. (1993) *Ancient Egyptians*. London: Watts/Gloucester.
Ganeri, A. (2001) *Egyptians*. London: Aladdin/Watts.
Guy, J. (1998) *Egyptian Life*. Tunbridge Wells: Ticktock Media.
Harris, N. (1995) *Mummies*. London: Watts.

Harrison, S. (1990) *Egypt*. London: BBC.
Hart, G. (1990) *Ancient Egypt*. London: Dorling Kindersley.
Kerr, J. (1990) *Egyptian Farmers*. Hove: Wayland.
Malam, J. (1991) *Indiana Jones Explores Ancient Egypt, Ancient Egypt Resource Book*. London: Evans.
Mason, J. (1991) *The Tomb of Tutankhamun*. London: Longman.
McNeill, S. (1996) *Ancient Egyptian People*. Hove: MacDonald/Young.
McNeill, S. (1996) *Ancient Egyptian Places*. Hove: MacDonald/Young.
Morley, J. (1993) *Egypt in the Time of Rameses II*. London: Simon & Schuster.
Parker, J. (1996) *Pyramids and Temples*. London: Belitha Press.
Reid, S. (1993) *Ancient Egypt*. London: Belitha Press.
Shuter, J. (1991) *Ancient Egyptians*. Oxford: Heinemann.
Shuter, J. (2001) *Ancient Egypt*. Oxford: Heinemann.
Sims, L. (2000) *A Visitor's Guide to Ancient Egypt*. London: Usborne.
Stead, M. (1985) *Ancient Egypt*. London: Evans.
Steele, P. (1994) *Egyptians and the Valley of the Kings*. London: Zoe Books.
Steele, P. (1995) *I Wonder Why Pyramids Were Built*. London: Kingfisher.
Steele, P. (1997) *Find Out About Ancient Egypt*. London: Southwater.
Steele, P. (1998) *My Best Book of Mummies*. London: Kingfisher.

For teachers

BBC *Egypt, Programme 1: Gift of the Nile* (video). London: BBC.
Brown, S. (1998) *Ancient Egypt*. Coventry: Prim-Ed Publishing.
Elding, S. (1995) *Ancient Egypt*. Dunstable: Folens.
Masson, N. *et al.* (1983) *Primary Language Programme, Book 2*. Oxford: Heinemann.
Purkis, S. (2000) *A Sense of History – Key Stage 2 Ancient Egypt Teacher's Book*. London: Longman.
Qualifications and Curriculum Authority (QCA)/ Department for Education and Employment (DfEE) (2000) *Update of History Schemes of Work*. London: QCA.
Wallace, B. (ed.) (2001) *Teaching Thinking Skills Across the Primary Curriculum: A practical approach for all abilities*. London: David Fulton Publishers in association with NACE.
Wilson, E. (1986) *Ancient Egyptian Designs*. London: British Museum Publications.

Using the TASC Problem-solving Model to Explore Artefacts

JOY BENTLEY

Developing historical study with artefacts can support students in their grasp of difficult concepts and can bring life to a wide variety of topics. It is an exciting way to encourage close observation, investigation and interpretation. Often quite ordinary artefacts (a salt dish or a postcard, for example) can link children to historical understanding and exploration of change.

In the Programme for Study in history for Key Stages 1 and 2, the pupils should be taught:

KS1

- to find out about the past from a range of sources of information, for example, stories, eye witness accounts, pictures and photographs, artefacts, historic buildings and visits to museums, galleries and sites, the use of ICT-based sources;

- to ask and answer questions about the past.

KS2

- how to find out about the event, people and changes studied from an appropriate range of sources of information, including ICT-based sources, for example, documents, printed sources,

CD-ROMs, databases, pictures and photographs, music, artefacts, historic buildings and visits to museums, galleries and sites;

● to ask and answer questions, and to select and record information relevant to the focus of the enquiry.

Teaching the skills of history is very much supported by the TASC Problem-solving Model. The Wheel lends itself readily to a creative exploration of artefacts, while at the same time encouraging a structured approach and scaffolding the students' exploration and learning.

The use of artefacts has been used across both key stages successfully, the demand and detail being linked to the ability range of the pupils. The sessions described in this chapter have allowed for a greater depth of exploration of artefacts than is often pursued by teachers adhering to QCA exemplars, but such an enhanced time allocation gives benefits by encouraging:

● skills of observation

● interpretation of evidence

● communication

● collaborative skills.

Artefacts study, however, does provide some concerns for teachers:

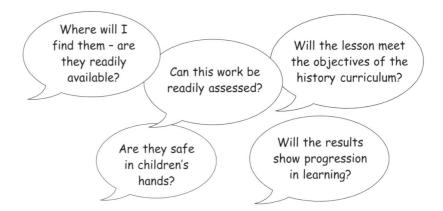

REFLECT　How often do you plan for the use of artefacts?

Can you see opportunities to weave them into your medium-term planning at times other than when a loan happens to be available from the museum or gallery?

The majority of QCA history units (QCA/DfEE 2000) suggest the use of artefacts as necessary resources, for example:

- **Unit 1**

  'How are our toys different from those in the past?' suggests the use of a selection of toys dating from 1950s to the present day.

- **Unit 3**

  'What were seaside holidays like in the past?' suggests the use of artefacts and souvenirs from seaside holidays in the past.

- **Unit 6**

  'Invaders and settlers' would include the use of pictures of objects/artefacts, archaeological finds/video.

- **Unit 8**

  'What were the differences between the lives of rich and poor people in Tudor times?' suggests the use of postcards and pictures of Tudor houses and portraits and replicas of artefacts from museum loan collections.

- **Unit 9**

  'What was it like for children in the Second World War?' suggests the use of information about the impact of the war on everyday life, e.g. pictures, newspapers, posters and ration books.

- **Unit 11**

  'What was it like for children living in Victorian Britain?' suggests the use of information on Victorian children at work, contemporary engravings, extracts from factory and mine reports and information on Victorian schools, e.g. school log books and inspection reports.

PURPOSE

In this chapter we describe some of the experience of teaching historical skills with artefacts. The main purpose is to provide an exemplar which can be applied to any aspect of history being taught – whether QCA exemplars or school generated units: the methods employed can be used in isolation or as additional support within a unit. The exploration of the TASC Wheel with artefacts took a number of lessons in the form outlined here, but the Wheel is flexible and can be made to fit a variety of time structures.

The pupils involved cover almost the whole of KS2, from Year 3 to Year 6 and it was important to give the children detailed experience of the TASC strategy from the beginning of the unit of work. The practical nature of the activities and the need for collaboration provided an excellent vehicle for embedding the Wheel.

It is possible that you feel that the history curriculum is 'full' but by giving more time initially to developing efficient thinking skills, you will encourage more independent and effective historians.

Working with TASC

Through the following studies, the children were encouraged to:

● become more familiar with assessing artefacts – by posing questions

● use the artefacts to make historical connections – a catalogue was produced for the 'sale' of the artefacts and timelines were constructed

● understand that artefacts have a value today – a 'Bargain Hunt' scenario was enacted

● transfer the use of a common artefact to the present day – effective advertisements were designed for milk bottles.

Each of these activities is described in more detail below. At the end of this chapter you will find some more suggested activities for using artefacts in various QCA history study units.

Exploring artefacts in the classroom context

COMMENT ▶

The children were used to grouping for enquiry projects and also used to having flexible working groups according to the intended outcome. It was explained that there would be a variety of end products linked to the artefact activities. The organisation of the learning would also be flexible but largely through:

● role play

● extended writing

● posing questions

● developing depth in questioning

● designing advertisements to influence.

Pupils began by gathering and organising ideas about what they already knew about the artefact being observed by the group. The aim was to provide an artefact not already recognised by the group. The more advanced the class the more difficult it was to find unusual artefacts – Victorian washing dollies and such were a no go area!

The children were encouraged to:

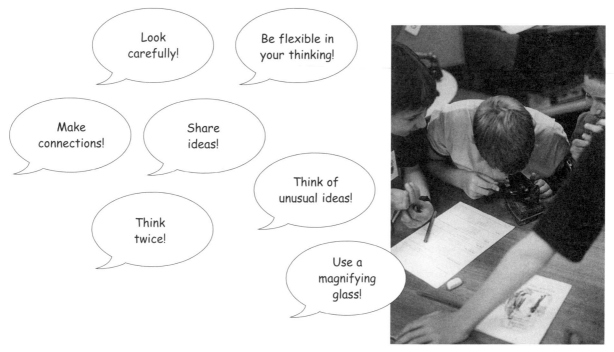

Cooperative investigation

The children discussed how they could record the questions they wanted to ask. Some remembered the radial grid they had used in literacy studies linked to history. They set about recording the questions to which they required answers on an individual basis. Invariably they filled the grid and their questions dealt with physical aspects such as materials used, colour, roughness, sharpness. But through teacher modelling the children extended their thinking to develop in-depth questions.

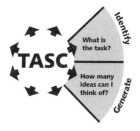

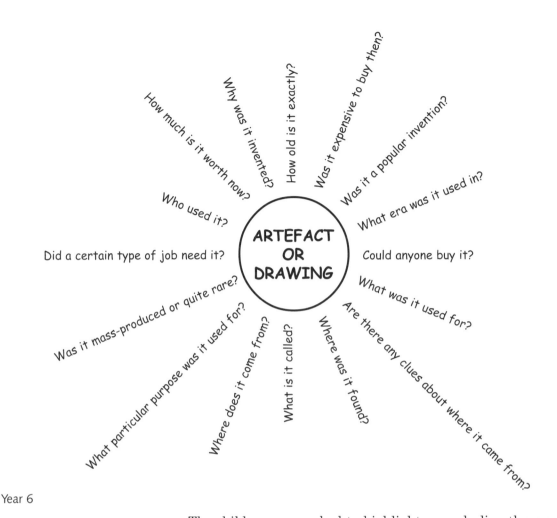

How much is it worth now?

Why was it invented?

How old is it exactly?

Was it expensive to buy then?

Was it a popular invention?

Who used it?

What era was it used in?

Did a certain type of job need it?

ARTEFACT OR DRAWING

Could anyone buy it?

Was it mass-produced or quite rare?

What was it used for?

What particular purpose was it used for?

Where does it come from?

What is it called?

Where was it found?

Are there any clues about where it came from?

Year 6

The children were asked to highlight or underline those questions they felt were the most important in giving them a wider picture of when and by whom the artefact was used.

Working on the radical questioning grid

A blank grid was then given to each group and group members were asked to collaborate to decide on the group's key questions.

Some groups prioritised the order of their research and their key questions.

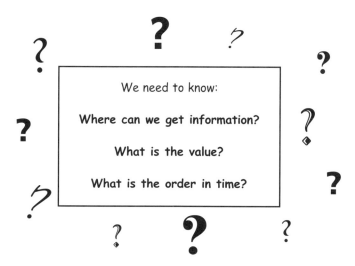

We need to know:

Where can we get information?

What is the value?

What is the order in time?

The new grid was then completed by the group and the decision-making and reflection was intensive at times. The opportunity to use desk microphones should not be missed if the class is used to this form of recording. It allows the sharing of good collaborative thinking with the rest of the class – it is sometimes hard to recreate the excitement and spontaneity of the original thinking when you ask the group to share their thoughts in a plenary session.

Having come to a consensus for the shared questions grid, the children were asked to further refine their thinking by highlighting the six most important questions to them – questions which would lead their research to discover more about the artefact.

It's also a good idea to ask the children to extend their ideas using the categories below:

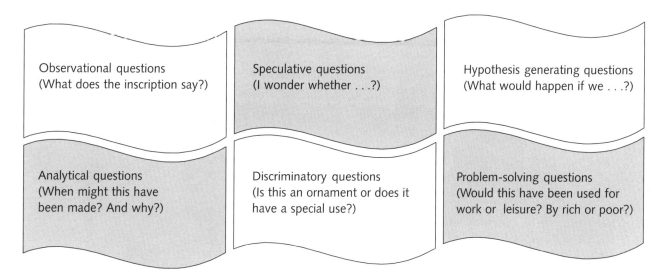

Observational questions
(What does the inscription say?)

Speculative questions
(I wonder whether . . .?)

Hypothesis generating questions
(What would happen if we . . .?)

Analytical questions
(When might this have been made? And why?)

Discriminatory questions
(Is this an ornament or does it have a special use?)

Problem-solving questions
(Would this have been used for work or leisure? By rich or poor?)

 In general, the children showed no constraints in their questioning because we deliberately tried to create a 'safe climate' where they could venture their opinions. They really began to speculate and talk in detail about their ideas.

 What would you suggest are the features of such a 'safe climate'?

 The groups then shared their artefacts and the main key questions they had selected. Here the teacher's role was to act as the oral historian and provide some degree of background for the artefact, making sure that the minimum information is given – just enough to get them really interested! Of course, if the project was limited for time the 'oral historian' could offer the answers sought by the children.

The children then searched for answers to the key questions of the group through using a range of research strategies and sources, including:

DOCUMENTS BOOKS PICTURES CD-ROMS

LETTERS WEBSITES/INTERNET POSTCARDS LIBRARY

STORIES MUSEUM CATALOGUES CONTEMPORARY BOOKS/DOCUMENTS NEWSPAPERS

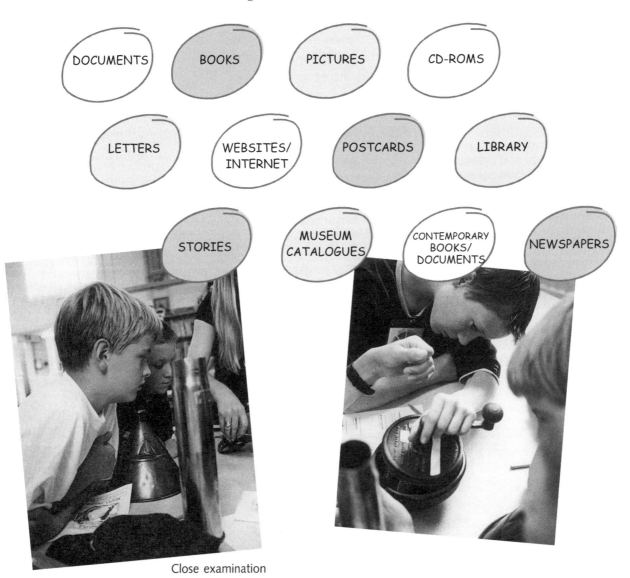

Close examination

We used the **implement** segment of the TASC Wheel in order to make use of the researched information: the aim was to provide a further context for communicating the discoveries. The children decided to produce an auction catalogue since some groups had already explored these when working on their artefacts. We prioritised what we needed to do.

Antiques catalogue

▼

Price guide

▼

Who owned the artefact?

▼

Picture

▼

Description

▼

Cover design

Let's think about an aspect of extension for a moment!

In order to make full use of the children's research, the catalogue was used as a vehicle to promote some extended writing. It was also used as an avenue for the children to empathise and hypothesise in terms of writing a biography of the owner(s) of the artefact: including why the artefact had been bought and why it had been sold. This brought out some very creative thinking and humour from some of the children!

glove stretcher
'owned by Lady Largehand, lady in waiting to the Queen on snow-balling outings'

flat iron
'owner driven insane by ironing her mother's nightdress 208 times until it was perfect'

bean cutter
'owner, John Eatalot, died from just too many beans'

The Bargain Hunt game

COMMENT ▶

We used the TASC Problem-solving Wheel to considerable effect when developing an understanding of how the value of artefacts can change over the years. The idea of using the TV *Bargain Hunt* programme as a stimulus for looking at change in history and empathy skills was appropriate in that:

● it provided a setting

● it allowed pupils to further examine artefacts in the present day setting

● it encouraged adventurous thinking

● it developed the awareness that artefacts can decline or appreciate in value

● it was fun!

Playing the game

A short clip from the TV programme was shown to familiarise the children with the object of the game.

Rule changes were:

● Only £50 to spend

● Must 'buy' at least four artefacts

● Group must agree on what was to be purchased.

Preparation included:

● Setting up artefact/antique stalls/flea market. (You can use pictures/postcards/photocopies of artefacts/digital photographs or on-screen presentations of artefacts if you need to 'pad out' your stock!)

● Producing £50 of cards, which were folded to stand, in denominations of £10, £5 and £1. (Each set was on different colour card or in different colour print to denote various groups in the class.)

● Preparing (but not revealing) a list of purchase prices against each artefact.

● The groups visited the 'antique market' and then returned to base to discuss what to buy with their £50.

● When consensus was reached they placed their money cards next to the artefact they wished to buy (some artefacts would have more than one card as other groups might choose to buy the same object).

● When all the spending was completed – each group submitted their list of purchases and the results were revealed to the class.

● The winning group was the one whose purchases matched today's asking price, i.e. the prices on the prepared list.

The results brought a great deal of interesting discussion on:

● why an artefact had a value today

● what its value had been when it was made

● how the artefact would be used today

● how collecting artefacts can become a hobby.

Learn from experience

What have I learned?

How well did I do?

Evaluate

TASC

The children reflected with insight on their learning.

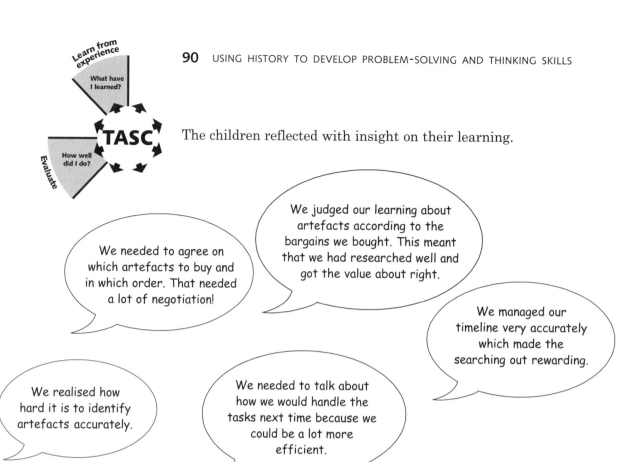

We needed to agree on which artefacts to buy and in which order. That needed a lot of negotiation!

We judged our learning about artefacts according to the bargains we bought. This meant that we had researched well and got the value about right.

We managed our timeline very accurately which made the searching out rewarding.

We realised how hard it is to identify artefacts accurately.

We needed to talk about how we would handle the tasks next time because we could be a lot more efficient.

COMMENT ▶

We followed the same procedures when we did an exploration of **irons** and **milk bottles**.

● We used a collection flat irons, plug irons, coke irons, gas irons and electric irons. The task was to develop a chronological timeline and the children presented an exhibition with explanation cards for the rest of the school.

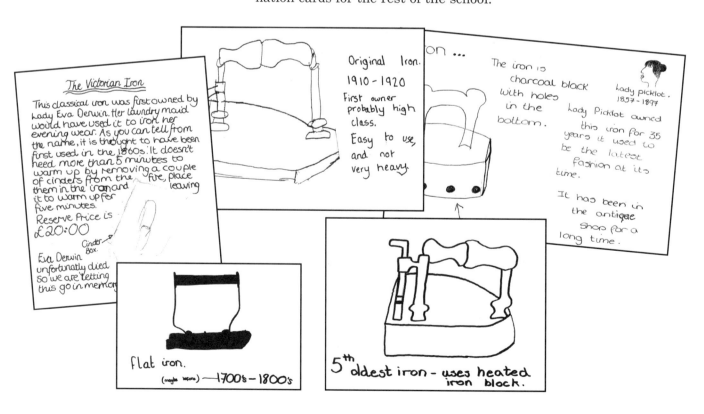

● Milk bottles make a fascinating study! The task was to study the range of advertising on a selection of milk bottles and then to design a new milk bottle with modern advertising. The range of bottles we studied had adverts including Disney characters, cereals, drinks, health messages, police information. The children were keen to produce their own adverts and were very influenced by environmental concerns. Designs of milk bottles and advertisements were displayed for the rest of the school.

Organising the display

Redesigning milk bottles

Main points for our milk bottle advert

Needs few words
Strong colour
Good slogan!
A rhyme?
Funny?

What would happen if we ban milk bottles?

It's pointless!
Dairies will go out of business
Disabled people won't be able to go out to get milk
Milkmen will lose their jobs
We won't have an easy supply
Some people might stop drinking milk
Some lonely people won't be able to talk to the milkman
Milkmen bring other things like butter, bread and eggs
It's a British tradition!
The milkman wakes us up!

Conclusion

The study of artefacts had indeed provided opportunities for the development of the skills of enquiry and interpretation. The children demonstrated:

● their enthusiasm to engage in thinking about history

● their awareness of the complexity of discussing artefacts

● the 'fickleness' of fashion and pricing!

● an interest in searching for artefacts as a hobby

● an interest in other people's lives.

The study of artefacts, importantly, gave the children the chance of developing their 'learning how to learn' skills. They learned how to structure their enquiry, how to work systematically through stages of planning and implementation. Most important, perhaps, was their realisation that history is an avenue for thinking and problem-solving.

Pages 94–95 provide an overview of the artefacts project.

Suggested activities for using artefacts in QCA history study units

---

ACTIVITY FOR UNIT I

How are our toys different from those in the past?

Collect two sets of toys, one set from around 1950 and the other from the present day. Ask the pupils to record the characteristics of each group separately on Post-it notes. Then ask the pupils to arrange their Post-it notes into a Venn diagram showing similarities and differences. Groups report back to the rest of the class about the reasons for their grouping.

(Note: The whole year group can gather collections of toys so that there are sufficient toys for them to work in groups.)

Ask the pupils to design the ideal toy which incorporates all the common characteristics shared by the 1950s' toys and the present day toys.

Groups generate ideas for their ideal toy design. Then each individual pupil can choose which toy they prefer and say why they have made their particular choice.

Each child can draw or make their ideal toy and show/demonstrate it to the rest of the group.

Each group can evaluate the effectiveness of their individual designs and justify the criteria they used for judging.

Pupils arrange an exhibition of their work including their thinking and planning sheets organised in 'concertina' booklet format.

Pupils discuss what they have learned about the characteristics of interesting toys and why children need toys. They also discuss how they worked as a group.

Artefacts and enquiry: a way to good thinking skills in history

KS2, 2c/d, 3, 4a/b, 5a/b/c

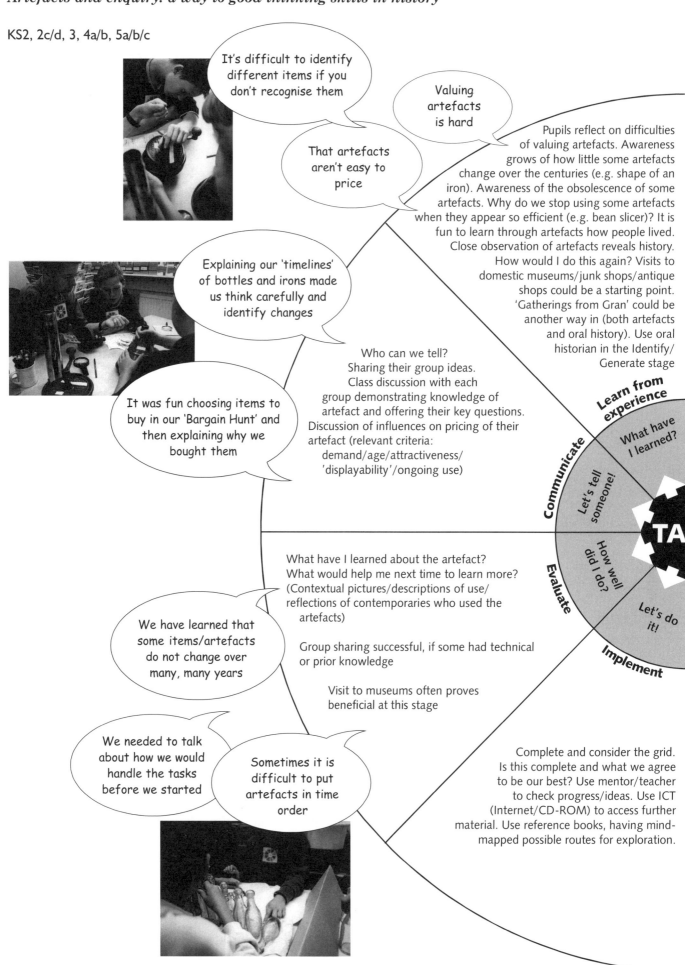

It's difficult to identify different items if you don't recognise them

Valuing artefacts is hard

That artefacts aren't easy to price

Pupils reflect on difficulties of valuing artefacts. Awareness grows of how little some artefacts change over the centuries (e.g. shape of an iron). Awareness of the obsolescence of some artefacts. Why do we stop using some artefacts when they appear so efficient (e.g. bean slicer)? It is fun to learn through artefacts how people lived. Close observation of artefacts reveals history. How would I do this again? Visits to domestic museums/junk shops/antique shops could be a starting point. 'Gatherings from Gran' could be another way in (both artefacts and oral history). Use oral historian in the Identify/ Generate stage

Explaining our 'timelines' of bottles and irons made us think carefully and identify changes

Who can we tell? Sharing their group ideas. Class discussion with each group demonstrating knowledge of artefact and offering their key questions. Discussion of influences on pricing of their artefact (relevant criteria: demand/age/attractiveness/ 'displayability'/ongoing use)

It was fun choosing items to buy in our 'Bargain Hunt' and then explaining why we bought them

Learn from experience

What have I learned?

Communicate

Let's tell someone!

TA

Evaluate

How well did I do?

Let's do it!

Implement

What have I learned about the artefact? What would help me next time to learn more? (Contextual pictures/descriptions of use/ reflections of contemporaries who used the artefacts)

Group sharing successful, if some had technical or prior knowledge

Visit to museums often proves beneficial at this stage

We have learned that some items/artefacts do not change over many, many years

We needed to talk about how we would handle the tasks before we started

Sometimes it is difficult to put artefacts in time order

Complete and consider the grid. Is this complete and what we agree to be our best? Use mentor/teacher to check progress/ideas. Use ICT (Internet/CD-ROM) to access further material. Use reference books, having mind-mapped possible routes for exploration.

Reproduced with permission from Wallace, B. and Bentley, R. (eds) (2002) *Teaching Thinking Across the Middle Years: A practical approach for children aged 9–14*. London: David Fulton Publishers in association with NACE.

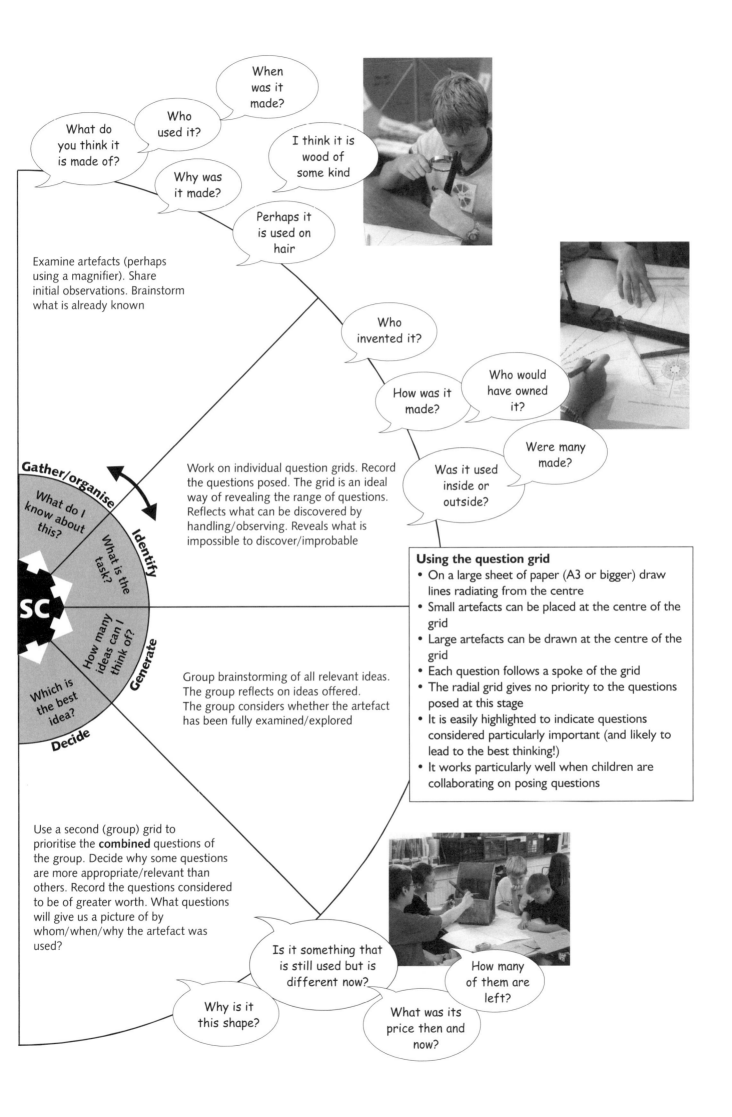

When was it made?

Who used it?

What do you think it is made of?

Why was it made?

I think it is wood of some kind

Perhaps it is used on hair

Examine artefacts (perhaps using a magnifier). Share initial observations. Brainstorm what is already known

Who invented it?

How was it made?

Who would have owned it?

Was it used inside or outside?

Were many made?

Work on individual question grids. Record the questions posed. The grid is an ideal way of revealing the range of questions. Reflects what can be discovered by handling/observing. Reveals what is impossible to discover/improbable

Gather/organise

What do I know about this?

Identify

What is the task?

SC

How many ideas can I think of?

Generate

Which is the best idea?

Decide

Using the question grid
- On a large sheet of paper (A3 or bigger) draw lines radiating from the centre
- Small artefacts can be placed at the centre of the grid
- Large artefacts can be drawn at the centre of the grid
- Each question follows a spoke of the grid
- The radial grid gives no priority to the questions posed at this stage
- It is easily highlighted to indicate questions considered particularly important (and likely to lead to the best thinking!)
- It works particularly well when children are collaborating on posing questions

Group brainstorming of all relevant ideas. The group reflects on ideas offered. The group considers whether the artefact has been fully examined/explored

Use a second (group) grid to prioritise the **combined** questions of the group. Decide why some questions are more appropriate/relevant than others. Record the questions considered to be of greater worth. What questions will give us a picture of by whom/when/why the artefact was used?

Is it something that is still used but is different now?

How many of them are left?

Why is it this shape?

What was its price then and now?

ACTIVITY FOR UNIT 3

What were seaside holidays like in the past?

 Collect artefacts, souvenirs and photographs about seaside holidays in Victorian times and in the present time. Provide each group with a collection of mixed items. Ask the pupils to group the artefacts and photographs into 'then and now' sets. Let each group make a list of the characteristics of each of their 'then and now' sets and justify their sets.

 Let the pupils choose from one of the following activities:

● Generate ideas for a brochure to advertise a Victorian seaside holiday.

● Generate ideas for seaside holiday activities of the future.

● Generate ideas for designs of bathing costumes for Victorian children, modern children and children of the future.

 Let the pupils decide on their choice of activity: they can make and decorate a holiday brochure in Victorian style; design and make a model of their futuristic seaside activity; or design sets of cardboard cut-outs with paper bathing costumes and set them against the appropriate background.

 Let the children gather in appropriate activity groups and decide on one aspect to praise and one aspect which could be improved for each item they have made.

 Each group can create a display for another class and present a summary of their findings in any format they choose.

 Hold a class discussion about why people need holidays and what makes an enjoyable holiday. This could be recorded in mindmap form and used as a stimulus for writing.

ACTIVITY FOR UNIT 8

What were the differences between the lives of rich and poor people in Tudor times?

---

1. Ask the class to generate broad headings for comparing rich and poor people of today, e.g. houses, clothing, etc. Let each group organise the headings as a mindmap on a sheet of A1 paper and fill in details under each broad heading.

2. Provide pictures of various kinds of Tudor clothing, houses, streets, artefacts, museum replicas if possible and video clips. Ask the pupils to draw up a mindmap, parallel to number 1 above, of life in Tudor times. Let the pupils supplement this comparison with their own research.

Ask the pupils to discuss in groups and decide with reasons whether it was an easier life if you were to be 'poor' in Tudor times or 'poor' today.

Take feedback from the whole class and scribe their comments in two columns onto a large sheet of A1 paper. Ask the groups to prioritise a list of hardships from 'most hard' to 'least hard'. Let them present their ideas in a chart format.

Organise for each group to present their findings to another class.

Discuss these questions with the class:

● What have you learned about life in Tudor times?

● How clearly have you presented your ideas?

● How well did you work as a group?

Ask each group to generate a list of reasons why life has improved for the ordinary people of today. Then ask the children to draw up a list of reasons why they think that life has not improved. This work can be used as the stimulus for argumentative writing.

ACTIVITY FOR UNIT 9

What was it like for children in the Second World War?

 This is a wonderful opportunity to bring senior citizens into the school to work with the children. Together, they can set up a display of artefacts such as pictures, photographs, newspapers, posters, gas masks, ration and clothing coupon books, etc.

 Let the children decide which activity they want to pursue, e.g. write and perform a play; make a recording of music then and now; find out about jazz and jitterbugging and perform some routines; write a rap song to portray then and now; research old films; compare and contrast the cost of living during the war and today, etc.

 The pupils can devise a questioning framework and interview the senior citizens, research on the Internet, and/or visit a local museum.

 Using the TASC Wheel to guide their work, pupils can plan and carry out their projects in groups, keeping a diary of their discussions and decisions.

 Let the pupils organise their own performance or exhibition and construct a questionnaire for the audience to fill in with regard to their critical evaluation of the children's work. The children can analyse the questionnaires using pie charts, line graphs or block graphs.

 The pupils will have acquired an extensive range of information which can be used as the stimulus for discussion about the feelings of people who lived through the Second World War. This knowledge and understanding can also be used as the stimulus for letter-writing, poetry, diaries, songs, etc.

Note: A similar kind of activity could be developed for **Unit 11** (What was it like for children living in Victorian Britain?). Possible projects on the Victorians include: comparing schooling then to that of today using artefacts such as school logbooks and inspection reports; working conditions using factory and mine reports; old-time music hall using photographs and songs; diet using cookery books, etc.

Resources

Corbishley, M. (ed.) (1990) *Learning from Objects: A teacher's guide.* London: English Heritage.

David, R. (1996) *History at Home: A guide for parents and teachers.* London: English Heritage.

Durbin, G. (1989) *Using Portraits: A teacher's guide.* London: English Heritage.

Fines, J. and Nichol, J. (1997) *Teaching Primary History.* Oxford: Heinemann Educational Publishers.

Hall, C. (1989) *Evidence Starters.* Glasgow and London: Blackie and Sons.

Lawrie, J. and Noble, N. (1990) *Victorian Times.* London: Unwin Hyman.

Pressley, A. (1999) *The Best of Times: Growing up in Britain in the 1950s.* London: Michael O'Mara Books.

Qualifications and Curriculum Authority (QCA)/Department of Education and Employment (DfEE) (2000) *Update of History Schemes of Work.* London: QCA.

Sampson, J. (1992) *Victorian Britain: Teachers' Resources.* Aylesbury: Ginn History.

The Schools' Library of Historical Source Materials, Long House, Church Road, Wisbech St Mary's, Cambs.

Starting History: Project Pack – Children (1991) Leamington Spa: Scholastic Publications.

Starting History: Project Pack – Leisure (1991) Leamington Spa: Scholastic Publications.

More Examples of TASC Extension Projects in History

TRICIA MCLEAN, RICHARD SCOTT (YEAR 5/6) SELECIA CHAPMAN (YEAR 5/6) AND SHEILA WOODHEAD (YEAR 4)

The following examples of history projects show how groups of teachers and their pupils have used the TASC Framework to structure their planning and thinking.

A. Projects developed by Tricia McLean and Richard Scott

Year 5 and 6: Gonerby Hill Foot CE Primary School, Lincs.

As a whole school we had been introduced to the TASC Problem-solving Wheel and then as a staff we had trialled a range of techniques with all the children in our classes, sharing ideas and results over several twilight sessions. As a development from this initial work, we elected to work in-depth on a number of history projects with a group of our most able pupils using the TASC Problem-solving Wheel to guide our exploration. We were working in unknown territory in a way! We wanted to see how far these very able children could progress using the complete range of TASC problem-solving and thinking skills. The intention was that we would later contribute to an in-service training day for other schools, sharing our experience and exhibiting the children's work.

Consequently, we selected a group of Year 5/6 children who would meet one afternoon a week for ten weeks. We knew the children well and knew that some of them could work at speed and in depth and could easily make up the work missed in the two hours out of the regular classroom every week. In the group we also included some pupils who we suspected were coasting and 'doing the stint', and some who were butterfly minded and who found it difficult to concentrate for any length of time.

We were a little anxious and we were not quite sure where we would start. But we welcomed the opportunity to explore a new approach in detail and with depth. We were not sure how prescriptive we should be. We decided to take the children's ideas on board and to let the children lead us. We would intervene when necessary: we would act as facilitators and, in a way, follow where the children led us and reflect back their thinking with questions for further thought.

The group decided that they wanted to work in three smaller subgroups to explore aspects of one of the following topics:

- Group1: **The Second World War**
- Group 2: **The Vikings**
- Group 3: **Local history**

Although the lesson planning for these topics is outlined here, it is important to realise that the children developed their own projects guided by the TASC Wheel: their projects evolved as they identified the steps they needed to take. They kept careful records of their planning and decisions so that when they reflected on the whole experience, they referred to the TASC Wheel and could easily recall the detail of what they had done, how effectively they had learned, and what they would change and improve the next time.

ACTIVITY PLAN

Group 1: The Second World War

Collect all the ideas relating to what the children already know about the Second World War, then ask them to organise the random points into sections according to topics and sub-headings. Devise a questionnaire to find out more information and identify people in the community who could be interviewed. The Internet provides extensive information, but the children need to be selective and only extract what is relevant.

Identify the task of writing and producing a play.

Ask the group to generate the storyline of the play and show it in a flow chart format – then as a comic strip in order to identify the scenes. Brainstorm the characters, recording in key words in the form of star charts together with possible speech, costumes and music.

Draft and re-draft the play, decide on the venue and audience, rehearse and perform the play to the rest of the school.

Provide the audience with evaluation cards so that they can provide feedback on their reaction to the play. Use the debriefing discussion to enable the children to reflect on what and how they have learned and what they would change next time.

ACTIVITY PLAN

Group 2: The Vikings

 Let the children create a mindmap of what they already know about Viking longboats then brainstorm additional questions to bridge the gaps in their knowledge. Divide the research areas up between them and give them a specified time to look for the information they need.

 Guide the children to consider a number of key issues: How was the frame constructed? What materials were used? What were the exact measurements? What scale should we work to? Then, if necessary, allocate further, more specific and detailed research tasks among the group.

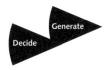 Let the children work in groups to generate ideas for the construction of the Viking longboat and then to make prototypes to trial various materials. They need to be guided to calculate important angles, identify key structures, work to scale, enlarge specific sections of plans and photographs.

 The completed model should be accurate and checked against drawings, plans and photographs. In particular, the children need to check the prototype of the rib cage and discuss possible adjustments to angles and key joints. Some changes might have to be made in the materials used.

 Let the learners exhibit their models of the longboat with information cards to explain the structure and how they made it. Then they can possibly take the models to a nearby museum where they can be displayed.

 The children should identify their most important learning points and discuss how they would approach a similar major construction task. They need to analyse the mistakes they made and think about how they would avoid similar mistakes next time.

ACTIVITY PLAN

Group 3: Local history

Collect all the knowledge the children already have about the local area. Ask the children to group the ideas, identify the gaps in what they know, what they need to find out and how they will conduct the research. Let the group allocate research tasks among themselves and report back to each other.

Ask the group to decide how they will present their ideas to the rest of the class. Let the group discuss the pros and cons of their suggestions. (After much discussion, the group finally decided to produce an information booklet.)

Let the group think about ideas for the information booklet and decide on the most important information to be included. Then ask the children to decide on the general layout and the visual format. This involves analysing a range of information booklets as well as generating their own ideas.

As the children to plan the production of their booklet, allocating tasks appropriately. (The group decided to produce the final version of the booklet using PowerPoint together with a visual software package.)

Discuss a possible market for the sale of the booklet and organise the procedure.

Ask the pupils to devise an evaluation format to give them feedback on the success of their booklet. Also ask them to produce a flow chart of their procedure with notes about the setbacks as well as the successes. Discuss what they learned about the way they worked and how they could improve next time.

We began by revisiting the TASC Wheel and the pupils decided that, firstly, they needed to **gather and organise** what they already knew. They used the TASC symbols they had already designed to monitor the way they worked.

The initial gathering of ideas roamed widely and the children decided that it was necessary to group the ideas in some way. They realised that collectively they knew a great deal already but they also realised that they needed to decide which avenue they would explore further and for what purpose.

So they needed to decide on the end product – the task they would work towards. This would enable them to decide what further questions they needed to ask, what additional information they needed and how they would research that information.

Thinking with the TASC Wheel

Looking for more information

Group 1: The Second World War

Group 1, comprising girls only, decided to produce a play about the feelings of a family during World War II when their father goes to the war. This was a difficult point to manage because they wanted to rush ahead and gather costumes and make-up before thinking about the purpose and content of their play. The lure and excitement of dressing up was too strong for them to pause and think clearly about their goal first! At this point, we needed to intervene and refer to the stages of the TASC Wheel and analyse the importance of **gathering** more information and **generating** ideas before **deciding** on a plan and **implementing** their decision. Consequently, the children realised that they didn't understand what it was really like to live in a time of war. They decided to design a questionnaire to interview a number of elderly people so that they could extend their knowledge and understanding before generating the story and exploring the characters who would be in their play.

Main teaching point

We needed to guide them into working in greater depth with a fuller understanding of the conditions of the time and the feelings of the family.

Group 2: The Vikings

Group 2, a group of boys and girls, decided to build a Viking boat. They had found a picture and wanted to gather bits of building material to make any old boat. All they were concerned about was the outward appearance and the thrill of making and painting it. We needed to intervene by letting them assume that we knew nothing about Viking boats, developing their questioning skills by modelling questions such as:

What were Viking boats made from?   How were they made?

Did they use skilled craftsmen?   Did they have plans?

The children caught the questioning and were soon asking their own questions:

How long did they take to build?   How big were the boats?
How did they get the rounded shape?   Did they have maps?
How stable were they in the water?   How fast could they travel?
How did they fasten the boat together?   Did they make a frame first?
How did they get their food and water?   Should we work to scale?
How many people could sail in them?

Main teaching point

Our questioning intervention led them to work in greater depth and with more understanding of the issues involved in the making of a Viking boat.

Group 3: Local history

Group 3 consisted of boys only, one very able boy being the dominant member, used to quick success, and very popular on the sports field. This boy had already decided what 'his' group would do. He had borrowed a book on Margaret Thatcher (the local person of repute) and wanted to summarise the story of her life and photocopy pictures from the book. The rest of the group wanted to produce a newspaper. It took a lot of exploring and negotiating: firstly, the fact that summarising and copying from one book was an easy option; and secondly, that producing a newspaper was a huge task for the time we had to complete the project. We wanted the decision to be the children's so we spent time helping them to focus on the need for quality of the task together with an appropriate time-scale. They finally decided to produce an information booklet about the Grantham area which they could sell to the local museum and library! It helped to clarify the task and also to motivate them by suggesting that possibly they could present their project using PowerPoint. Incidentally, the boys had never used PowerPoint before but had absolutely no problems in mastering the techniques and using it creatively and competently.

Main teaching point

Our intervention had encouraged the group to dismiss the easy option of summarising from one book, also to be realistic about the time they had available and to focus on a manageable project which had quality, depth and entrepreneurial attraction.

Examples of pupils' work

Group 1: The Second World War

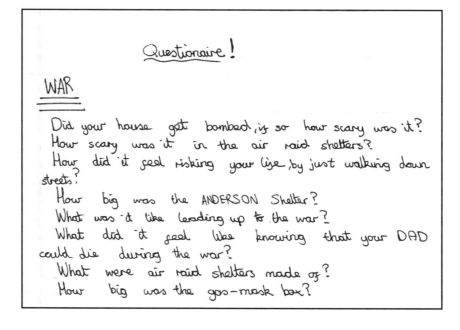

History in the 1930s: What do we know?

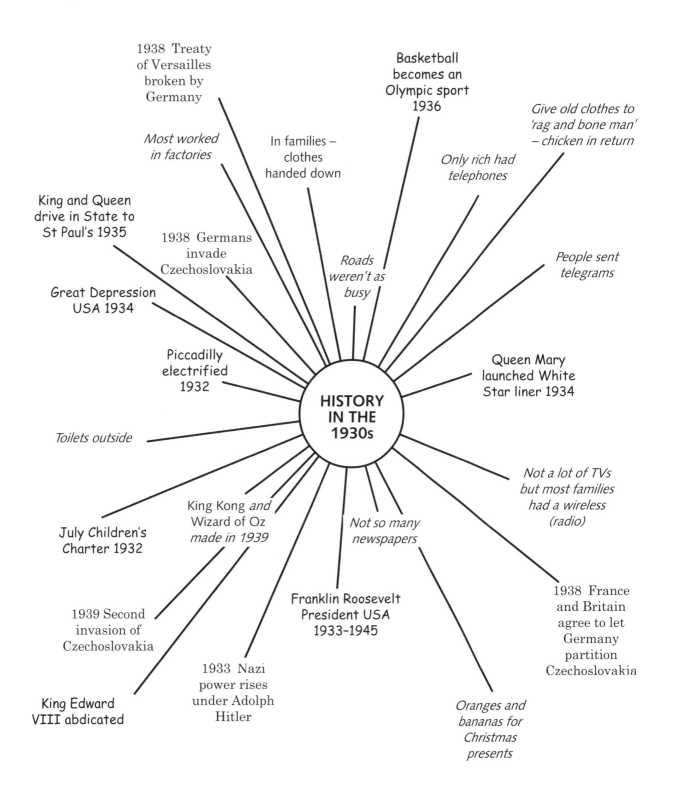

1938 Treaty of Versailles broken by Germany

Basketball becomes an Olympic sport 1936

Give old clothes to 'rag and bone man' – chicken in return

Most worked in factories

In families – clothes handed down

Only rich had telephones

King and Queen drive in State to St Paul's 1935

1938 Germans invade Czechoslovakia

Roads weren't as busy

People sent telegrams

Great Depression USA 1934

Piccadilly electrified 1932

HISTORY IN THE 1930s

Queen Mary launched White Star liner 1934

Toilets outside

King Kong and Wizard of Oz made in 1939

Not so many newspapers

Not a lot of TVs but most families had a wireless (radio)

July Children's Charter 1932

1939 Second invasion of Czechoslovakia

Franklin Roosevelt President USA 1933-1945

1938 France and Britain agree to let Germany partition Czechoslovakia

King Edward VIII abdicated

1933 Nazi power rises under Adolph Hitler

Oranges and bananas for Christmas presents

Key (differentiated by font)

Germans
Other important world events
Everyday life in the war years

Extract from the script

KIDS: Help! What are we going to do?

MUM: Don't worry! We've practised the routine for an air raid plenty of times! Come on! Gasmasks on! Into the Anderson Shelter! Now! Move!

EM: Mum, I'm scared! What's going to happen to us? What about our house?

DOT: Mum! Are we going to die? What if we get bombed on?

MUM: (*With uncertainty and anxious look on her face*) Please, just stay calm! We won't die . . . (*She whispers to herself*) I hope!

Group 2: The Vikings

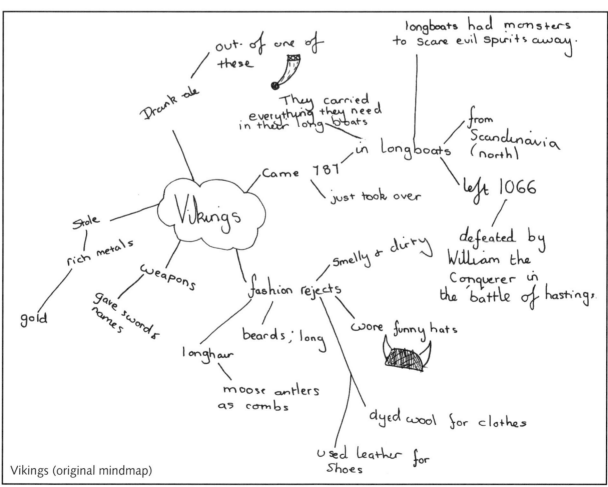

Vikings (original mindmap)

Plans of boat

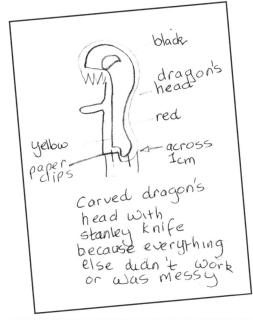

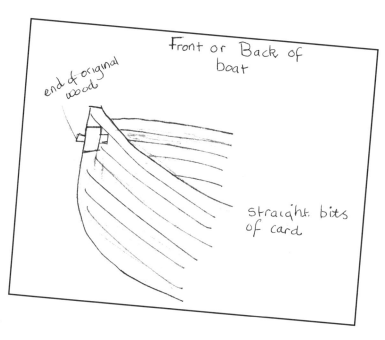

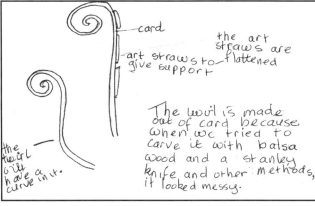

Making the Viking boat

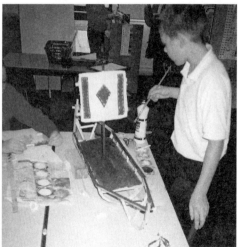

The finished boat

Group 3: Local history

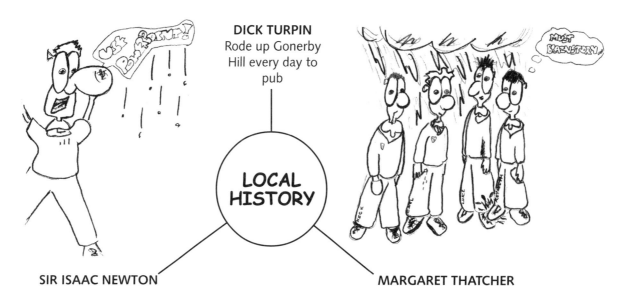

DICK TURPIN
Rode up Gonerby
Hill every day to
pub

LOCAL HISTORY

SIR ISAAC NEWTON

Statue inaugurated – Sept 1858

Lived in village nearby

Went to King's School

Engraved his name on windowsill

Discovered gravity

Born at Woolsthorpe, Lincs at the
Manor House, 25 Dec 1642

Trinity College Cambridge

Lived in London

When born so weak and small –
unlikely to survive

When he was three his mother remarried

Isaac brought up by his grandmother

Lonely man, good scholar

Took time off school to run farm but
daydreamed about maths

Uncle put him back in school

1660 went to Trinity College Cambridge

Studied philosophy and science

MARGARET THATCHER

Head of KGGS (Kesteven & Grantham
Girls School)

Name before married – Margaret Roberts

Main Hall in KGGS was named Roberts' Hall

Lived above a shop – Roberts' Grocery Stores,
1 North Parade, Grantham –
now Living Health

Primary School – Huntingdon Road

Born 13 October 1925

Read Chemistry at Cambridge

1946 became President of the University
Conservative Association

13 Dec 1951 married Dennis Thatcher

Studied Law and graduated 1953

Gave birth to twins 1953, Mark and Carol

Member of Parliament for Finchley 1959

1961-1964 Joint Parliamentary Secretary
Ministry Pensions and National Insurance

1964-1974 – involved in Education

1979-1990 First woman PM

Key (differentiated by font)

What do we know already?

What did we find out?

Local history mindmap

Making a decision tree

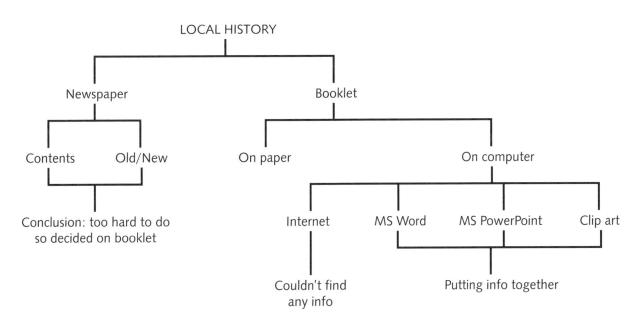

Local history booklet

REFLECT

What did we learn about the children?

- In working with the TASC Wheel as a framework for thinking, the children realised that their end product was better because they had worked in greater depth with a better understanding of the issues involved and the thinking processes they were using. We could see the thinking processes becoming automatic as they recognised opportunities for using them.

- Their enthusiasm grew as they became engrossed in their tasks and we were bombarded throughout the weeks with requests for extra time to be spent on the projects. The children worked voluntarily during morning and lunch breaks and a great deal of work was done in their own time.

- At first, the pupils were not used to working collaboratively. They were used to working 'in groups' but on separate individual assignments. They were not used to sharing ideas and negotiating decisions as a group. However, given the opportunity, they quickly learned how to work as a team especially, we think, because we drew their attention to the need for cooperative planning and the delegation of tasks among the group.

- The children could handle depth and complexity and could work with amazing speed when they were given the chance to do so and when they were motivated by the task.

- They could cope with a tight time schedule once they had clarified their goals and planned how they would work as a team.

- The groups not only realised the importance of planning the way they worked but also the importance of planning who would undertake the research and what areas each person would cover. They could see the waste of time involved in everyone researching the same things.

- The greatest realisation was, perhaps, their discovery that they could achieve well beyond the target they set themselves.

What did we learn about ourselves as teachers?

- We realised that children respond very positively when they have ownership of their task through making their own decisions about what and how they will learn. We need to accommodate the opportunity for them to do this more often.

- We could see how these very able learners were too used to skating over content, getting quick but superficial results, choosing the easy route rather than going for the challenge. We need to expect far more from such pupils and we need to provide in-depth resources.

- The pupils were too used to being organised and told what to do: they initially expected to be spoon-fed but responded so readily when we reflected the decision back to them.

- When we introduced different recording styles, the children responded to the slogan 'Maximum thinking and minimum recording'.

- Although the children enjoyed decision-making, they needed guidance in order to clarify their goals and plan an efficient way of working.

- Next time, we will give more emphasis at the beginning to the criteria for judging the success of the task.

- We realised the importance of setting clear goals at the end of each session for what we wanted to achieve by the beginning of the next session.

- The children were able to reflect on their thinking processes and to modify their thinking procedures accordingly. They found the TASC diagram (see p. 17) which gave them access to 'thinking language' very useful for talking about their thinking activities.

The following flow charts give a summary of the children's processes of working, together with their comments and reflections.

 REFLECT

As you read the children's records of their thinking, note how:

- they take control of their own planning and use their initiative to organise their work;

- willing they are to revise their procedures in order to learn more efficiently;

- they recognise the gaps in their knowledge and take steps to remedy this;

- ready they are to give extra time to the projects;

- they are able to reflect on their thinking and suggest ways for improving next time.

We've learned: how to use the TASC Wheel to guide our thinking and a lot about what happened to ordinary people in the 1940s.

We know a lot about the Second World War.

I like working in a team. When you split the jobs up, you get a lot more done.

It's good to work with friends.

We learned how to sort out arguments. Sarah helped us to do that.

When we work together we have a lot of ideas.

The result is better. Four brains are better than one!

When you look ahead and know what you are doing, you work harder.

I like working like this because I think more.

You realise that you know more than you think you do.

We learned a lot about organising and planning so that things went smoothly.

I really felt frightened and sad as though I was the character. I could imagine how scared the girls felt and how happy they were to hear that their father was safe.

It was interesting to talk to people who could remember what it was like. It was much more interesting than reading about it in a book.

It's important that children today know about the Second World War because we should know how much people suffered then.

It was no good thinking we could just dress up, we had to really know a lot about the times.

Doing history like this, you realise that history is about real people like us. You learn about their feelings and can imagine what they thought.

Doing everything ourselves, we had to think and work well together. And it was exciting to share what we knew with the rest of the school.

We presented our play to the whole school. I was nervous but because we had found out so much, I was able to act my part as though I was really there at the time.

How have I changed?
What do I think and feel now?
How else can I use what I've learned?
How would I do this again?

Who can I tell?
How can I tell or present?
What should I say?
How can I explain?
How do I interest someone else?
Do I have the right information?

What have I done?
Could I do it better next time?
Did I solve the problem?
Did I work as well as I could?
Would I do it differently next time?
Did I work well in my group?

Learn from experience
What have I learned?
Let's tell someone!
Communicate
How well did I do?
Evaluate
Let's do it!
Implement
TA

How do I check my progress?
Am I doing this correctly?
Is my plan working?
What do I do next?

We will know if the play is good because audience will applaud.

Will display all our work to show thinking and planning.

We will know how we feel about it – if we are satisfied.

Will make cards with 'very good', 'OK' and 'not very good' and ask Year 5 and Year 6 to fill them in. We would also fill in the cards and show results in a graph.

We need to photocopy script and learn the lines.
We thought about the characters:

I'm Emma. I'm a twin to Dot. I'm moody but I can be nice sometimes.

I'm Mum, Anna Jones. I'm very caring. I'm quite stressed when my husband goes to the war. I'm 33-years-old. I'm a housewife. I try to keep calm.

I'm Val. I'm 13-years-old. I'm a schoolgirl and I'm quite clever. I care about my sisters. I'm very organised.

I'm a 'mardy' child. I'm bossy and I hate my sisters. I'm Dot. I'm 12-years-old.

We need to do a lot of rehearsal at home. We need to know each other's lines. Mr Riches is going to film it.

Our History Project: The Second World War
Using the TASC Wheel to guide our thinking

We thought we didn't know much at first.

When we shared what we knew, we knew a lot!

Made a questionnaire for Mrs McLean's parents and Mrs Brown – they helped a lot.

Went on the Internet and found out more.

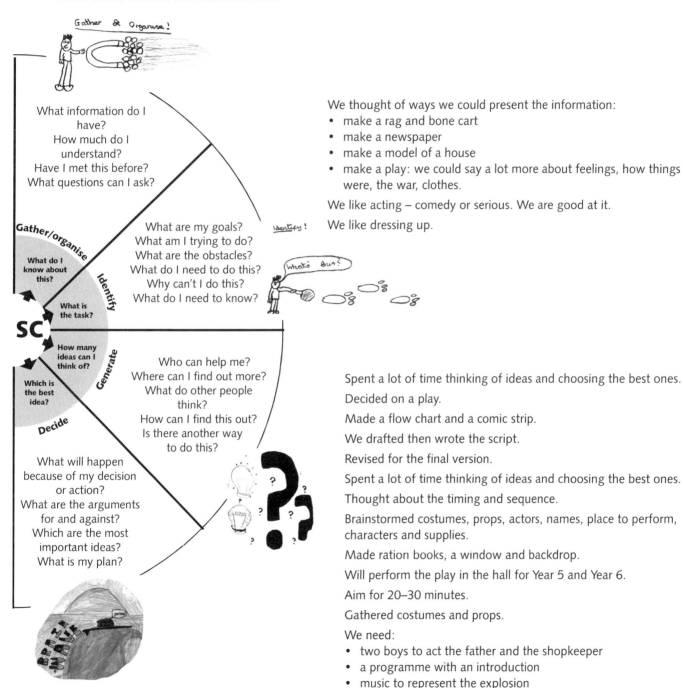

Gather & Organise!

What information do I
have?
How much do I
understand?
Have I met this before?
What questions can I ask?

What are my goals?
What am I trying to do?
What are the obstacles?
What do I need to do this?
Why can't I do this?
What do I need to know?

Identify!

What's this?

Gather/organise

What do I
know about
this?

Identify

What is
the task?

SC

How many
ideas can I
think of?

Generate

Which is
the best
idea?

Decide

Who can help me?
Where can I find out more?
What do other people
think?
How can I find this out?
Is there another way
to do this?

What will happen
because of my decision
or action?
What are the arguments
for and against?
Which are the most
important ideas?
What is my plan?

We thought of ways we could present the information:
- make a rag and bone cart
- make a newspaper
- make a model of a house
- make a play: we could say a lot more about feelings, how things
  were, the war, clothes.

We like acting – comedy or serious. We are good at it.

We like dressing up.

Spent a lot of time thinking of ideas and choosing the best ones.

Decided on a play.

Made a flow chart and a comic strip.

We drafted then wrote the script.

Revised for the final version.

Spent a lot of time thinking of ideas and choosing the best ones.

Thought about the timing and sequence.

Brainstormed costumes, props, actors, names, place to perform,
characters and supplies.

Made ration books, a window and backdrop.

Will perform the play in the hall for Year 5 and Year 6.

Aim for 20–30 minutes.

Gathered costumes and props.

We need:
- two boys to act the father and the shopkeeper
- a programme with an introduction
- music to represent the explosion
- background music.

We really made a longboat in the style of the Vikings.

Tackled problems.

We solved the problems as a team.

It all took a long time and we worked very hard.

We would do it better next time because we have learned from experience.

We know more about the Vikings' building method.

We are more experienced at DT – planning, making, evaluating.

We work better as a team.

We know more about the Vikings and we will remember!

We are more confident to take on a similar task.

We'll use the TASC Thinking Wheel again.

You really need to plan carefully.

MOST IMPORTANT!

You have to get the main structure right first then fill in the details.

How have I changed?
What do I think and feel now?
How else can I use what I've learned?
How would I do this again?

Learn from experience

What have I learned?

Set up a display.

Made cards to show how we made the longboat.

Teachers took our work to their training day!

We are going to show it to the Jorvic Centre (local museum), parents/family and other classes.

Who can I tell?
How can I tell or present?
What should I say?
How can I explain?
How do I interest someone else?
Do I have the right information?

Communicate

Let's tell someone!

TA

Is it looking more like a longboat?

Reactions from classmates: looking good; It's taken a long time! Looks authentic!

Checked against plans.

We knew what the finished product should look like because of our research.

Checked rib structure with prototype.

IS IT WORKING? YES!

Decided to angle rib joints to give better shape.

Some ideas changed, better ones thought of.

Curve of bow and stem improved because changed materials (balsa to card).

Successfully completed.

Worked as a team.

What have I done?
Could I do it better next time?
Did I solve the problem?
Did I work as well as I could?
Would I do it differently next time?
Did I work well in my group?

Evaluate

How well did I do?

Let's do it!

Implement

How do I check my progress?
Am I doing this correctly?
Is my plan working?
What do I do next?

Colour of boat – brown, dark or light – authentic?

Argument about decking – R and C

Are card and wood needed? Would card suffice?

Design of sail

MOST IMPORTANT IDEAS

Methods and processes involved in making
Keel and ribs – main structure!
Wooden support for newly glued rib sections
Cardboard glued to joints to increase strength
Leaving glue to harden overnight before sticking together
Masking tape to aid initial gluing
Wooden supports for sail

Our History Project: The Vikings
Using the TASC Wheel to guide our thinking

What do we know about this?

We have heard some information before.

But it's difficult to recall the information.

The detail is hard to describe.

Other people's ideas helped to remind us.

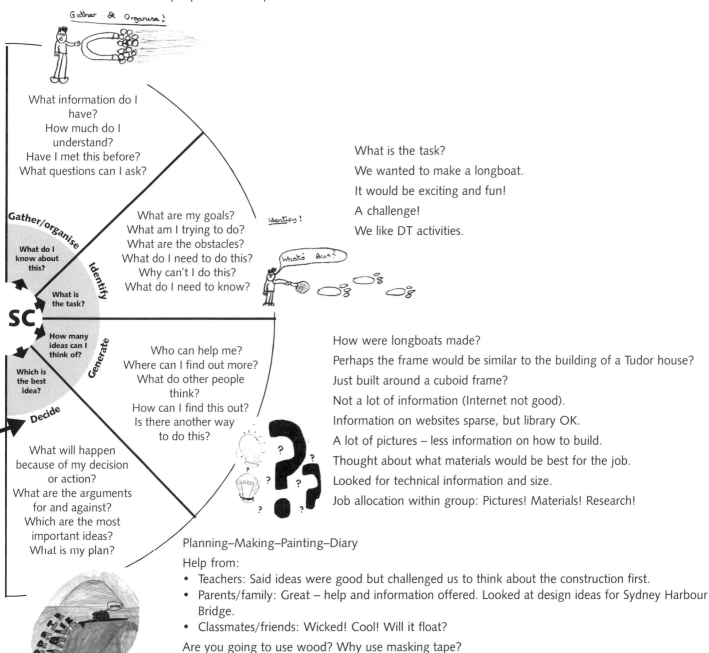

What information do I have?

How much do I understand?

Have I met this before?

What questions can I ask?

What is the task?

We wanted to make a longboat.

It would be exciting and fun!

A challenge!

We like DT activities.

What are my goals?

What am I trying to do?

What are the obstacles?

What do I need to do this?

Why can't I do this?

What do I need to know?

How were longboats made?

Perhaps the frame would be similar to the building of a Tudor house?

Just built around a cuboid frame?

Not a lot of information (Internet not good).

Information on websites sparse, but library OK.

A lot of pictures – less information on how to build.

Thought about what materials would be best for the job.

Looked for technical information and size.

Job allocation within group: Pictures! Materials! Research!

Who can help me?

Where can I find out more?

What do other people think?

How can I find this out?

Is there another way to do this?

What will happen because of my decision or action?

What are the arguments for and against?

Which are the most important ideas?

What is my plan?

Planning–Making–Painting–Diary

Help from:

- Teachers: Said ideas were good but challenged us to think about the construction first.
- Parents/family: Great – help and information offered. Looked at design ideas for Sydney Harbour Bridge.
- Classmates/friends: Wicked! Cool! Will it float?

Are you going to use wood? Why use masking tape?

We made a prototype.

We tried paint colours.

We tried garden canes for flag.

We looked at pictures and tested angles.

Scanned, and picked out relevant parts to enlarge.

Tried out different materials: card, wood, clay, playdough, straws.

Tried out different methods: card over playdough moulding/gluing.

Longboat of card, wood, glue wouldn't be able to go in water.

Won't be made of the same materials as Vikings used.

Our History Project: Local history
Using the TASC Wheel to guide our thinking

I learned about the history of Grantham.

We learned information from each other.

We argued about what to do. So we decided to do a booklet because we could mix our ideas.

We enjoyed putting everything together using PowerPoint.

We enjoyed using the 'effects'.

We found it difficult to find the information we needed on the Internet, so we went to the museum and the library.

We learned how to talk to an expert on local history.

We will all check the draft and revise.

I am going to add the bits on Grantham.

We will check the accuracy and if it really relates to Grantham.

I am going to add the index later.

We have appointed a final editor.

We will all judge the 'Clip art' and the 'Word art'.

We will take it to the Museum and the Library and ask what they think about it.

We will ask other pupils what they think of our booklet.

I am going to change grammar/spelling and add introductions.

Sell it?

How have I changed?
What do I think and feel now?
How else can I use what I've learned?
How would I do this again?

Who can I tell?
How can I tell or present?
What should I say?
How can I explain?
How do I interest someone else?
Do I have the right information?

What have I done?
Could I do it better next time?
Did I solve the problem?
Did I work as well as I could?
Would I do it differently next time?
Did I work well in my group?

How do I check my progress?
Am I doing this correctly?
Is my plan working?
What do I do next?

Learn from experience
What have I learned?
Communicate
Let's tell someone!
Evaluate
How well did I do?
Let's do it!
Implement
TA

We need to improve the grammar and punctuation.

We need to strengthen the connection to Grantham.

We need to add an introduction to explain chapters.

It's all going to plan, apart from some mistakes, which can easily be changed. We now need to work hard on these to finish it in time.

How can we work as a group?
• share out tasks
• C and K research and edit
• N and L research and scribe on to PowerPoint,

Locate books and PowerPoint.

Devise questionnaire for talk from Mr Thompson to cover: families, clothing, food, transport/roads, highwaymen, change in industry, buildings (e.g. Victorian, Georgian streets), and schools (Gonerby Hill Foot – late 1950s and St Sebastian's).

Go to Grantham library and museum to find out about: local schools, Margaret Thatcher (birth, life, school, college, parents, career) and Dambusters (time, where it was planned and attacks, Barnes Wallis's bouncing bomb).

Use PowerPoint so the front cover will be good and add pictures with Clip Art and Word Art.

Important ideas are:
• design of front cover
• contents (our plan: families, famous people, households, buildings, transport, sport, Dambusters)
• slides for information
• in chapters
• index.

What we already knew about Margaret Thatcher:
- Conservative Prime Minister
- previous surname was Roberts
- her father owned Roberts' Grocery store
- went to KGGS

What we already knew about Isaac Newton:
- famous local scientist
- gravity
- went to Kings School and engraved name

What we already knew about Dick Turpin:
- alleged to have travelled through area

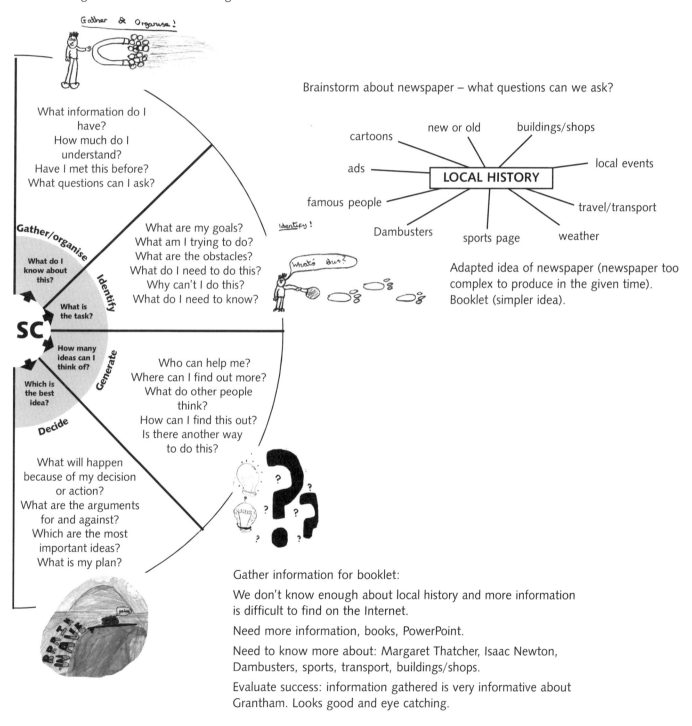

Gather & Organise!

What information do I have?
How much do I understand?
Have I met this before?
What questions can I ask?

Gather/organise

What do I know about this?

Identify

What is the task?

SC

How many ideas can I think of?

Generate

Which is the best idea?

Decide

What are my goals?
What am I trying to do?
What are the obstacles?
What do I need to do this?
Why can't I do this?
What do I need to know?

Identify!

What's this?

Brainstorm about newspaper – what questions can we ask?

cartoons   new or old   buildings/shops

ads   **LOCAL HISTORY**   local events

famous people   travel/transport

Dambusters   sports page   weather

Adapted idea of newspaper (newspaper too complex to produce in the given time). Booklet (simpler idea).

Who can help me?
Where can I find out more?
What do other people think?
How can I find this out?
Is there another way to do this?

What will happen because of my decision or action?
What are the arguments for and against?
Which are the most important ideas?
What is my plan?

Gather information for booklet:

We don't know enough about local history and more information is difficult to find on the Internet.

Need more information, books, PowerPoint.

Need to know more about: Margaret Thatcher, Isaac Newton, Dambusters, sports, transport, buildings/shops.

Evaluate success: information gathered is very informative about Grantham. Looks good and eye catching.

Conclusion

As we used the TASC Wheel, we became more confident and could see how it enabled us to work more efficiently. The processes of thinking became more important than the product, although the quality of the end product was far better that we had imagined it would be. We could see that although we spent more time in the beginning on introducing this way of working, the children became more efficient learners. All children would benefit from working in this way since the TASC Framework provides a scaffolding for them to manage their thinking; but able children also need to learn how to manage their way of thinking and working so that they become increasingly independent. Once they have the tools of 'learning how to learn', it becomes easier to set independent and small group assignments.

Importantly, the TASC Wheel can be used flexibly, either using the Wheel as a whole or using sections of it as opportunity and need arise. However, it is important that the pupils are aware of the processes underpinning the whole Wheel and that they also understand how it enables their problem-solving and thinking skills to improve. This group of bright children were conditioned by the repetitive nature of the National Curriculum and they were used to skating over the content rather than branching out on independent investigations of their own. We need to avoid that repetition by planning for such investigations as often as we possibly can. Very able children can work in much greater depth and breadth within the overall framework of the National Curriculum and they need the opportunities to do so.

B. Project developed by Selecia Chapman

Year 5 and 6: Billingborough Primary School, Sleaford, Lincs

I wanted the children to use the TASC Wheel as their thinking guide and I also wanted the activities to span across the multiple intelligences. We were going to explore aspects of the Tudors but I didn't want the children to repeat anything they already knew. I wanted them to work in depth on a range of aspects; I also wanted the children to take responsibility for their project and then to present their findings to the rest of the school.

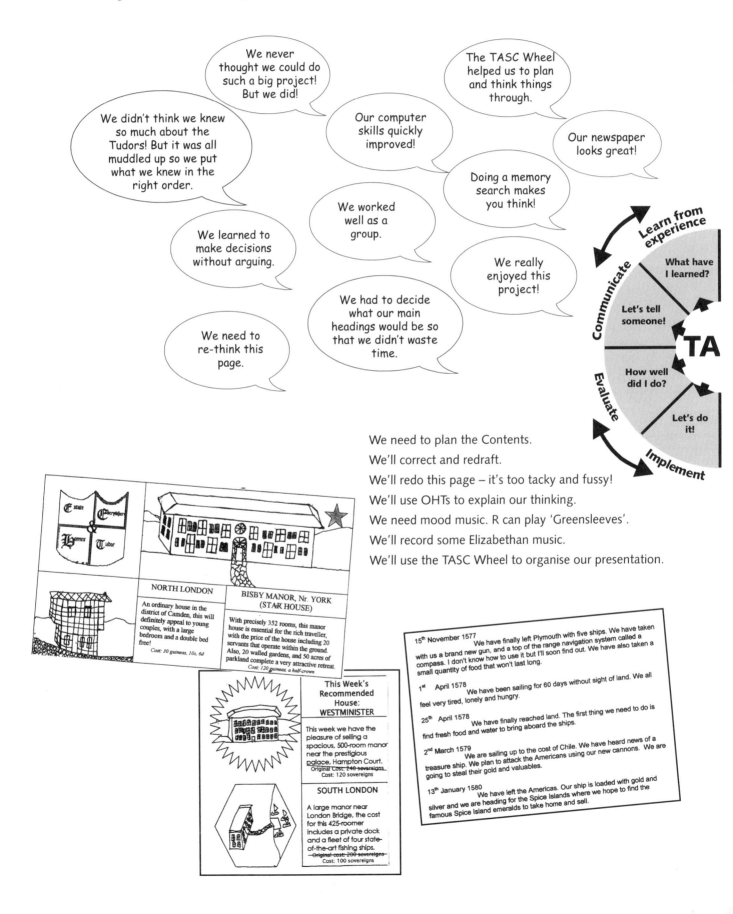

We never thought we could do such a big project! But we did!

The TASC Wheel helped us to plan and think things through.

We didn't think we knew so much about the Tudors! But it was all muddled up so we put what we knew in the right order.

Our computer skills quickly improved!

Our newspaper looks great!

Doing a memory search makes you think!

We worked well as a group.

We learned to make decisions without arguing.

We really enjoyed this project!

We had to decide what our main headings would be so that we didn't waste time.

We need to re-think this page.

We need to plan the Contents.

We'll correct and redraft.

We'll redo this page – it's too tacky and fussy!

We'll use OHTs to explain our thinking.

We need mood music. R can play 'Greensleeves'.

We'll record some Elizabethan music.

We'll use the TASC Wheel to organise our presentation.

NORTH LONDON

An ordinary house in the district of Camden, this will definitely appeal to young couples, with a large bedroom and a double bed free!
Cost: 30 guineas, 10s, 6d

BISBY MANOR, Nr. YORK (STAR HOUSE)

With precisely 352 rooms, this manor house is essential for the rich traveller, with the price of the house including 20 servants that operate within the ground. Also, 20 walled gardens, and 50 acres of parkland complete a very attractive retreat.
Cost: 120 guineas, a half-crown

This Week's Recommended House: WESTMINISTER

This week we have the pleasure of selling a spacious, 500-room manor near the prestigious palace, Hampton Court.
~~Original Cost: 240 sovereigns~~
Cost: 120 sovereigns

SOUTH LONDON

A large manor near London Bridge, the cost for this 425-roomer includes a private dock and a fleet of four state-of-the-art fishing ships.
~~Original cost: 200 sovereigns~~
Cost: 100 sovereigns

15th November 1577
We have finally left Plymouth with five ships. We have taken with us a brand new gun, and a top of the range navigation system called a compass. I don't know how to use it but I'll soon find out. We have also taken a small quantity of food that won't last long.

1st April 1578
We have been sailing for 60 days without sight of land. We all feel very tired, lonely and hungry.

25th April 1578
We have finally reached land. The first thing we need to do is find fresh food and water to bring aboard the ships.

2nd March 1579
We are sailing up to the cost of Chile. We have heard news of a treasure ship. We plan to attack the Americans using our new cannons. We are going to steal their gold and valuables.

13th January 1580
We have left the Americas. Our ship is loaded with gold and silver and we are heading for the Spice Islands where we hope to find the famous Spice Island emeralds to take home and sell.

The children

- already knew a lot
- were very enthusiastic and did a lot of work in their own time
- really took to mindmapping
- shared the research then reported back to each other
- enjoyed the planning on large sheets
- took charge of the display
- realised the need to narrow the focus
- consulted the TASC Wheel and used it to guide their planning
- were quite willing to re-think their ideas and to re-plan

What we found out

A timeline for the explorers – map of explorations – what is was like to be a sailor – how they navigated – what sailors ate and drank

Tudor games and sports – the apparatus they used – the rules of the games – whether we play any today

The clothes they wore – high fashion – rich and poor styles – how much they cost

Shakespeare's famous plays – how they were performed

A timeline for the Tudor kings and queens – the important things that happened

How Tudor houses were built – what they cost – how many are still present today

What do we already know?

Mary Rose

Henry VIII: lots of wives, obese, padded clothes

dissolution of monasteries

big houses

Spanish Armada

Christopher Columbus

Sir Frances Drake   explorers   hunting

Shakespeare

Elizabeth I   jousting

Globe Theatre

Greensleeves   feasts

Bartholemew Diaz

America   hurdy-gurdy

SC

Gather/organise

- What do I know about this?
- What is the task?

Identify

- How many ideas can I think of?
- Which is the best idea?

Generate

Decide

1. Let's make a newspaper to commemorate the death of Elizabeth I.
2. Let's act a section from *A Midsummer Night's Dream*.

1. Our newspaper

time chart   diary of a sailor

exploration   maps   mindmaps

comic strip   PowerPoint   cartoon   diagrams

games   dances   food   fashion   jewellery

houses   sports

2. Our play

Which one?   What part?

Comedy?

Modern language?
How long?

Like the Globe theatre?
Costume?

Modern dress?

We must make a plan first.

We must decide who plays which character.

1487-1488. Bartholomew Diaz discovered The Cape of Good Hope.

1492-1502. Christopher Columbus discovered the West Indies. He then made more voyages to Central and South America.

1497-1498. John and Sebastian Cabot discovered Nova Scotia and Newfound Land and also visited Greenland.

1497-1499. Vasco da Gama discovered the sea route to India.

SHAKESPEARE TONIGHT

Around 1595 the English playwright William Shakespeare wrote, *Romeo and Juliet* one of his greatest tragedies. The play, set in Renaissance Italy, tells the story of two "star-crossed lovers" who become the tragic victims of the enmity of their two families and their own rash misjudgements.

William Shakespeare is one of most well known playwrights in the world; his other Tudor plays may not have been so well known, but they are equally brilliant. Macbeth with its scary and frightening twists, Hamlet with its strange and dramatic scenes and a midsummer night's dream to name but a few. Shakespeare's plays were mainly performed in the great Globe theatre in London along with mimes and puppets.

Music was also a very important part of Tudor life whether at home or at church. People played instruments such as the lute, recorder, organ, flute, and virginals. These were all put into practise, used as the background of the plays of the Globe. The music was used to set the scene, as there was no painted backdrop. The sound would drift around the open-air theatre so that both the rich spectators in the raised galleries under thatched roofs and the poorer groundlings that wandered around the high stage could hear. William lived in a house in Southwark next to the bear garden.

the owner of the Pinta slipped from its socket. I believe this was deliberately caused by Gomez Rascon and the owner of the caravel Cristobal Quintero. Neither of these men wanted to make this voyage.

Thursday 9th.
The Pinta was able to reach Grand Canary this morning.

Friday 17th
Two weeks have passed since our departure from Palos and the crew has become restive.

Tuesday 4th September
Today we loaded and stored dried meat and salted fish and some fruits. The fruit will have to be consumed early, for it will spoil if the voyage is of 3 weeks duration

Wednesday 5th September
The ships have been loaded and all is ready for the voyage. It sunrise I will lift anchor to begin the journey westward.

C. Project developed by Sheila Woodhead

Year 4: Pinchbeck East Primary School, Spalding, Lincs

As a school, we felt that we needed to give more attention to the development of our children's writing skills. Hence the aim of this initial pilot project was to trial the use of TASC to develop writing skills through a study of history. The topic from the Programme of Study for history was the Romans. The pilot project would be evaluated and used as a base for further staff development.

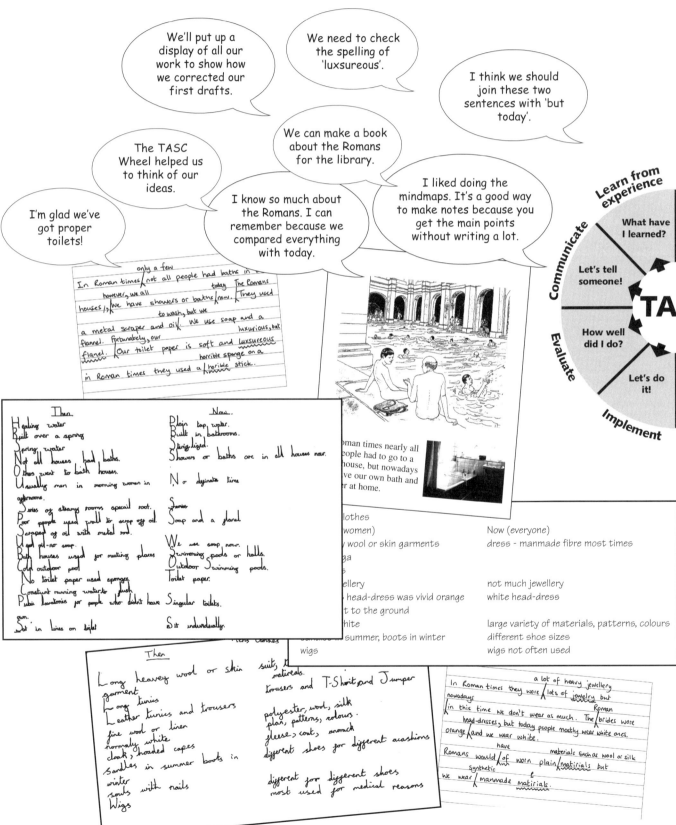

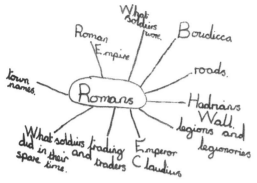

Romans

Roman Empire   roads

Hadrian's wall

legions and legionnaires

Emperor Claudius   trading

what soldiers did

town names   Boudicca   what soldiers wore

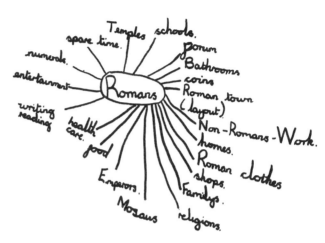

What would we like to know about?

temples   schools   forum   bathrooms   coins   Roman towns (layout)   non-Romans   work   Roman clothes   shops   families religions   mosaics   Emperors   food   health care   writing reading   entertainment   numerals   spare time

The three most interesting questions

1. What food did the Romans eat?

2. What was their health and hygiene like?

3. What clothes did they wear?

Teacher comment

The children worked enthusiastically developing their research skills, ICT skills as well as their writing skills. They worked in pairs to correct each other's work and wanted to spend extra time on their project. They also enjoyed the re-drafting process, discussing their improvements and using coloured pens to code-mark their corrections.

 **Learning Resources**

Further reading and textual resources

Andreetti, K. (1993) *Teaching History from Primary Evidence*. London: David Fulton Publishers.

Arnold, H. and Slater, L. (1999) *Victorians (9–11)*. Reading for Information Series. Leamington Spa: Scholastic.

Arthur, J. and Phillips, R. (eds) (2000) *Issues in the Teaching of History*. London: Routledge.

Ashby, R. and Lee, P. J. (1987) 'Children's concepts of empathy and understanding in history', in Portal, C. (ed.) *The History Curriculum for Teachers*. Lewes: Falmer Press.

Bage, G. (1999) *Narrative Matters: Teaching and learning history through story*. Lewes: Falmer Press

Bage, G. *et al.* (1999) *Classical History in Primary Schools, Teaching and Learning at Key Stage 2*. London: QCA Publications.

Bawden, N. (1973) *Carrie's War*. London: Victor Gollancz.

Blyth, J. E. (1988) *History 5–9*. London: Hodder and Stoughton.

Blyth, J. (1989) *History in Primary Schools*. Milton Keynes: OUP.

Blyth, J. and Hughes, P. (1997) *Using Written Sources in Primary History*. London: Hodder and Stoughton.

Body, W. (1998) *A World War 2 Anthology*. Harlow: Longman.

Bourdillon, H. (ed.) (1994) *Teaching History*. London: Routledge.

Castor, H. (2001) *Famous People, Famous Lives*. London: Franklin Watts.

Cooling, M. (1994) *Faith in History*. Guildford: Eagle.

Cooper, H. (1994) Chapters 5 and 8 in Bourdillon, H. (ed.) *Teaching History*. London: Routledge.

Cooper, H. (1995) *The Teaching of History in Primary Schools*, 2nd edn. London: David Fulton Publishers.

Counsell, C. and Thomson, K. (1997) *Life in Tudor Times*. Cambridge Primary History Series. Cambridge: Cambridge University Press.

Davies, J. and Redmond, J. (1998) *Coordinating History across the Primary School*. London: Falmer Press.

Department of Education and Science (1989) *The Teaching and Learning of History and Geography*. London: HMSO.

Department for Education and Skills (2001) *National Literacy Strategy: Framework for Teaching*. London: DfES.

Dickinson, A. K. and Lee, P. J. (1978) (eds) *History Teaching and Historical Understanding*. London: Heinemann.

Fines, J. and Nichol, J. (1997) *Teaching Primary History*. Oxford: Heinemann.

Frank, A. (1989) *The Diary of Anne Frank*. London: Pan Books.

Harnett, P. (1991) *Key Stage Two Teachers' Handbook*. Aylesbury: Ginn & Co.

Haywood, J. (1994) *The Romans*. Abingdon: Andromeda.

Hill, C. and Morris, J. (1992) *Practical Guides. History*. Leamington Spa: Scholastic.

Honey, A. (1992) *Investigating Family History*. London: The National Trust.

Hoodless, P. (ed.) (1998) *History and English in the Primary School*. London: Routledge.

Malam, J. (1994) *Indiana Jones Explores Ancient Rome*. London: Evans.

McAleavy, T. (1997) (series ed.) *Cambridge Primary History*. Cambridge: Cambridge University Press.

National Curriculum Council (1993) *Teaching History at Key Stage 2*. York: NCC.

Nichol, J. (1998) 'Nuffield Primary History: The Literacy Through History Project and The Literacy Hour', *Primary History* **20**, 14–17.

Place, R. (1993) *Clues from the Past*. Hove: Wayland.

Pluckrose, H. (1991) *Children Learning History*. Oxford: Blackwell.

Qualifications and Curriculum Authority (1998a) *Maintaining Balance and Breadth at Key Stages 1 and 2*. London: QCA.

Qualifications and Curriculum Authority/Department for Education and Employment (1998b) *History Teacher's Guide: A scheme of work for Key Stages 1 and 2*. London: QCA.

Qualifications and Curriculum Authority/Department for Education and Employment (2000) *Update of History Schemes of Work*. London: QCA.

Ross, S. (1997) *Please Help, Miss Nightingale*. London: Evans.

Sampson, J. *et al.* (1998) 'Learning the language of history; teaching subject specific language and concepts', in Hoodless, P. (ed.), *History and English in the Primary School*. London: Routledge.

Schools Curriculum and Assessment Authority (1997) *Planning the Curriculum at Key Stages 1 and 2*. London: SCAA.

Sellars, W. C. and Yeatman, R. J. (1973) *1066 and All That*. Harmondsworth: Penguin.

Tames, R. (1994) *What Do We Know About the Tudors and Stuarts?* Hemel Hempstead: Simon & Schuster

Triggs, T. (1990) *History in Evidence: Victorian Britain*. Hove: Wayland.

Westall, R. (1975) *The Machine Gunners*. London: MacMillan.

Wood, R. (1994) *Family Life in Victorian Britain*. Hove: Wayland.

Wood, R. (1994) *A Victorian School*. Hove: Wayland.

Wright, M. (1992) *A Really Practical Guide to Primary History*. Cheltenham: Stanley Thornes.

Historical games

'Chronology'. Gibsons Games Ltd (www.gibsonsgames.co.uk) manufacture under licence from the Great American Puzzle Factory Incorp., South Norwalk, Ct., USA.

'Egyptians'. Green Board Game Co. Ltd., 112A Cressex Business Park, Coronation Road, High Wycombe, Bucks.

'Nine Men's Morris'. Green Board Game Co. Ltd.

'Fox and Geese'. Green Board Game Co. Ltd.
'Historical Jigsaws'. Falcon Games, Hatfield, Herts.
'Historical Poster Puzzles'. Cheatwell Games, Lower Road, Chinnor, Oxford.
'World War II Spy'. Bags of Activity, McGraw Hill, 5–7 Pembroke Road, Water-beach, Cambridgeshire
'Cloister Games'. Historical Collections Gp PLC, Oxford Games Ltd, Oxford.
'Royal Game of Ur'. J. & L. Randall Ltd, Potters Bar.
'Historical Airfix Models'. Humbrol, Marfleet, Hull.
'Revell Historical Models'. (www.revell.de)
Board and Table Games from Many Civilisations. R. C. Bell. New York. Dover
  Publications.

The following offer on-line catalogues containing a range of products:
The National Trust (www.nationaltrust.org.uk)
English Heritage (www.english-heritage.org.uk)
The British Museum (www.britishmuseum.co.uk)
The Science Museum (www.sciencemuseum.org.uk)
The Victoria and Albert Museum (www.vam.ac.uk)
The Imperial War Museum (www.iwm.org.uk)

Some history websites

A walk through time www.bbc.co.uk/education/history/walk/
AHDS (Arts and Humanities Data Service) http://ahds.ac.uk:8080/ahds_live/
American and British History Resources www.libraries.rutgers.edu/rul/
  rr_gateway/research_guides/history/history.shtml
Ancient Egypt www.ancientegypt.co.uk
Archaeological Resource Guide for Europe http://odur.let.rug.nl/arge
Archaeology www.yorkarchaeology.co.uk
Archon (Archives on-line) www.hmc.gov.uk/archon/archon.htm
Archsearch http://ads.ahds.ac.uk/catalogue/
Argos http://argos.evansville.edu/

Battle of Hastings www.battle1066.com/index.html
BOPCRIS : Free archive of British official papers (1688–1995) http://
  www.bopcris.ac.uk/
British Archaeology www.britarch.ac.uk/ba/ba.html
British Humanities Index www.csa1.co.uk
British Museum http://www.thebritishmuseum.ac.uk/

Cadbury interactive website. Documents, photographs, references to Victorian
  Britain www.cadburylearningzone.co.uk
Calendars www.webexhibits.com/calendars/
Castles of Wales www.castlewales.com/home.html
Cathedrals www.bbc.co.uk/history/programmes/cathedral/map.shtml
Charles Booth On-line Archive (Documents and maps – life and labour of
  people in London 1886–1903) http://booth.lse.ac.uk/
Civil rights photographs www.civilrightsphotos.com
Compass: British Museum on-line http://www.thebritishmuseum.ac.uk/
  compass/
Council for British Archaeology www.britarch.ac.uk/index.html

English Heritage www.english-heritage.org.uk
Eureka www.eureka.org.uk

Fitzwilliam Museum www.fitzmuseum.cam.ac.uk

General Information www.britannia.com/history/

Historic Scotland www.historic-scotland.gov.uk
Historical Association (general and member information) www.history.org.uk

History Book Resources www.museums.com
History channel www.historychannel.com
History links www.historyonline.co.uk
History-net www.h-net.msu.edu
History resources www.ihrinfo.ac.uk
History's happening www.saber.net/~paloeser/
Horus history links www.ucr.edu/h-gig/horuslinks.html
Humbul (Humanities database) www.humbul.ac.uk

Institute of Field Archaeologists www.archaeologists.net/
International Bibliography of the Social Sciences www.bids.ac.uk

LSE Historical Pamphlet Collection www.library.lse.ac.uk/services/guides/
    pamphlets/british-history/

Manorial Documents Register www.hmc.gov.uk/mdr/mdr.htm
Museum of Antiquities Virtual Mithraeum http://museums.ncl.ac.uk/archive/
    mithras/intro.htm

National Curriculum Website www.nc.uk.net
National Museums and Galleries of Wales www.nmgw.ac.uk
National Railway Museum www.nrm.org.uk
National Register of Archives www.hmc.gov.uk/nra/nra2.htm
National Science Museum www.nmsi.ac.uk/education/stem/
National Science Museum Guide www.users.globalnet.co.uk/~weysci/
National Trust www.nt-education.org
Newseum Russia www.newseum.org/berlinwall/commissar_vanishes

On-line Reference Book for Medieval Studies http://orb.rhodes.edu/

Primary Schemes of Work www.open.gov.uk
Public Records Office www.pro.gov.uk
Public Record Office Virtual Museum http://www.pro.gov.uk//virtualmuseum/
    default.htm

QCA Publications www.qca.org.uk

Re:source www.resource.gov.uk
Resource guide for the social sciences www.jisc.ac.uk/subject/socsci/
Romans www.bbc.co.uk/education/romans/index.shtml
Royal Commission on the Ancient and Historical Monuments of Scotland
    www.rcahms.gov.uk/
Royal Commission on the Historical Monuments of England www.english-
    heritage.org.uk/

SCRAN (Scottish cultural resources) www.scran.ac.uk
Secrets of the Norman invasion (includes the Bayeux
    tapestry) www.cablenet.net/pages/book/index.html
SOSIG (Social Science Information Gateway) www.sosig.ac.uk/
Spartacus http://www.spartacus.schoolnet.co.uk

Tudors www.webpointers.com/henryviii.html www.maryrose.org/
    www.shakespeare4kidz.com/ and http://home.hiwaay.net/~crispen/tudor/
    index.html
24hour museum www.24hourmuseum.org.uk

Ulster Museum www.ulstermuseum.org.uk
United Kingdom Primary Documents http://library.byu.edu/%7Erdh/
    eurodocs/uk.html

Victoria Research web www.indiana.edu/~victoria/vwcont.html
Victorians www.victoriana.com www.nmsi.ac.uk/nrm/   and
    www.spartacus.schoolnet.co.uk
Virtual Mummy www.uke.uni-hamburg.de/institute/imdm/idv/forschung/
    mumie/index.en.html

Young Archaeologists Club www.britarch.ac.uk/yac/

 **Index**